Fearless At Any Cost

Paul Dobandi

08-06-18

TO: HILLARY

Paul Dobandi

authorHOUSE®

AuthorHouse™ LLC
1663 Liberty Drive
Bloomington, IN 47403
www.authorhouse.com
Phone: 1-800-839-8640

Published by AuthorHouse   09/17/2014

Book Cover designed by Artist Aranka Lackó

ISBN: 978-1-4567-6215-5 (sc)
ISBN: 978-1-4567-6214-8 (hc)
ISBN: 978-1-4567-6216-2 (e)

Library of Congress Control Number: 2011908111

For my family: my parents, brother, two sisters, and my daughters,
Claudia, Astrid, and Holly, and for my love, Sandi

I am also dedicating this book to all the people all around
the world who fearlessly fight and sacrifice their lives for
their freedom in the past, present, and future.

When the Going Gets Tough
(For my mother, from the prison)

Mother! I would like to sit one more time in your lap.
I'd like you to hold me one more time in your arms.
Protect me from cold winds and rain, and from
frightening nightly nightmares.

Mother! I have a wish to be a child again!
Please tell me fairytales!
I'm listening.
Rock me slowly to put me to sleep and then kiss me good night!
Mother! Painfully hard, my life!
Wishing for freedom, in replacement I get hard labor!
Too heavy the load …
Too heavy for my body and soul!
I feel the end for me is not that far!
Mother! Tears in my eyes!
Come, wipe them away, your son, I ask you;
Nag you, your son, screaming toward you for help!
Make me believe my hard life is only a bad dream!

Mother! I would like to sit one more time in your lap.
I like you to hold me one more time in your arms.
Protect me from cold winds and rain, and from
frightening nightly nightmares.

-Paul Dobondi

PART ONE: IN PRISON

Introduction

Darkness would take over the prison cell. It was not the darkness, though, that you welcomed in the idle minutes of the evening as you relaxed in your easy chair or lay in bed, giving well-deserved rest to your mind and body after a busy day.

No, this darkness didn't rock you to sleep; nor did it bring sweet, angelic dreams. This darkness did not bring a softly caressing mate whose fragrance would fill the night, who would whisper loving words into your ears.

No, this was the darkest of all darkness. Its generous presents were fear, fright, and nightmares given freely night after night. My teeth chattered and my eyes filled with tears every dark night. I was approaching the finality of a total mental breakdown.

Prison cell—many shrug off the idea with vacant eyes, and those are probably the better half of the population. Others might say, "Those in prison are there because they deserve it," or "Let them suffer in prison. Let them repent during those long years." But what about those innocents, the ones who suffer, fear every new day, and dread every approaching night? Those who try, with chattering teeth, to push the coming of the night out of their consciousness? Oh, God! The terrors of the night—the terrors of those longing for freedom!

The question of innocence, however, can be discussed later. For now, let's get back into the prison, where the innocent are sitting. All the cruelty, the fear, the sleepless nights, the beastly existence, everything considered evil happened to me, which put the final stamp on my youth. I can now safely commit to paper all the terror that was inflicted upon me. Should I do this? Is there reason to be afraid? Should I be wary? No! I am free now! All these things happened in Communist Romania. It is miserable, humiliating to spend your days in a prison cell in Romania. Even if you are lucky enough to get out sane, your first thoughts are of suicide. Yes! Suicide, to throw away the soiled flesh. Jump into a river—that should be good! The water might cleanse your dirtied body and soul. But what about your mind, your once crystal-clear thoughts?

Ah, forget the river; jump in front of a train! Let the train crush every last thought planted by the Communists. Yes, the train—that will be good. This would truly happen—the suicide, that is—if a loving person weren't there with her protecting hands. She is there, in that crucial moment, to prevent you from making the greatest mistake in your life. With her outstretched arms, she fights a mighty battle against the idea of suicide. It is hard to defeat the idea of suicide, so she keeps her eyes on you all the time, never letting you out of her sight. Minutes pass this way. You decided on suicide; she, the protecting fortress. Time passes, minutes to hours, hours to days. Then the days present you with more and more loving people who all join forces to battle the black thoughts of suicide, until they beat its last shadow out of your mind.

Finally, love conquers the dark thoughts. Love guides you back into the routine of everyday life. You continue your life living in happiness, and the sorrow, the worry it deals you daily, you contain with a deep, deep secret sigh, which you never dare to shape into a word. *Freedom*—this longing for freedom follows you everywhere. This word keeps on growing in you. It branches out, and oh, does it have flowers of sweet fragrance. The idea stays with you day and night. You whisper the word into your pillow, lest someone should hear it. Your whisper is so soft, you yourself might think it as a mere dream. But whether it is a dream or it is real, it is a cry for help. "God, help me! Oh, God, help me to escape from Communist Romania. God, please help me."

As you whisper this a thousand times a day, you shudder at every noise, worried that someone has heard your most secret prayer and squealed on you to the Communists. That would mean they would take over your mind again.

You stop trusting your friends, never knowing who will turn you in, and then you get back into *their* hands again. You will be back in the prison, where torture to your body and mind might rekindle the idea of suicide again.

CHAPTER 1

Sitting in prison, I had plenty of time to ponder over the events that had happened so fast. Did someone turn me in? Who likes to lick Communist asses? I thought my plan to sneak through the Romanian border to Hungary was flawless; still, the Romanian border patrol caught me. Did I make a mistake? Or was it the dark hand of fate? Who knows? I might never know.

For the rest of my life—if I ever make it out of here alive—I will be marked in the eyes of the Communists, a marked sheep destined for the slaughterhouse, food on someone's table. They'll tear me up, bite into me, scratch me till I bleed. Like hungry wolves, they'll bare their fangs and scream into my ears: "You worthless, insolent traitor! You anti-Communist filth! You disease-spreading maggot!"

It was easy enough to feel confident on my first day in prison. I soon found out, however, that six months in a Communist prison can fairly compare to ten years in any other prison.

The next day, my fate started to teach me this new math, where six can be more than ten.

We were roused in the cell with a painfully loud clambering noise. In case you didn't wake up fast enough to this unique, unrelenting sound, the beastly voice of the guard was suddenly louder than the alarm. Fright, as well as surprise, was my first reaction.

"Hey, you dirty beast, you trash of a traitor, get up, or I'll drum the wake-up call in your head!"

Since my head was already beaten badly enough, I got up in a real hurry, lest he fulfill his promise and drum the call on my head. I got up hurried to breakfast. Or, rather, I would have hurried, if the guard hadn't slapped me on my neck, so that I fell back into the cell. He hollered to explain.

"You idiot! What do you think, I am going to clean up after you? And don't forget, because I'll tell you only once. From now on, every morning, you take that wooden barrel, whether there is anything in it or not, and follow your comrades!"

I wasn't used to that, so I didn't even realize that the wooden barrel in the corner was supposed to serve as a toilet. There you go, civilization for you. Take the barrel, empty or full, every morning. How humiliating. Having no choice, I picked up the empty barrel and followed my prison mates. I tried to imitate their actions, since they seemed to be quite experienced in carrying their waste. I felt goose bumps on my back as I thought about doing this every morning for six months. I resolved to get used to it. You can get used to the stink of the skunk, too, if you try hard enough; eventually, it becomes just another smell. Besides, I did not have a choice. I had to get used to it. The worst part was, it had to be done before breakfast.

After cleaning, breakfast. My first breakfast in prison. Another surprise. God Almighty! I write down the menu, in case someone on the outside might want to adopt it. You will have to be sure to get a license from Romania though, for I am sure it has been patented. The menu, then: tea, in the likeness of bath water, although a laboratory check might have proven it otherwise. Who would really care? If they call it tea in the prison, then tea it is. Case closed. Next was a slice of bread. Unsurpassable; the best bakers in the world would fail in trying to recreate its quality. Its color would present a real challenge to any painter who tried to reproduce it: it started at a dark brown, shaded into pale, and then mixed with some gray. In the center of the slice, a small piece of rock was eyeing me. The prisoner could have no reason to complain. With his slice of bread, he also got a piece of the rock. On top of everything, the bread was speckled with green mold. The mold didn't alarm me much. I remember, a doctor friend of mine once told me—when I was on the outside, still eating white bread— that the mold on the bread is a type of penicillin, so why should I complain about getting my antibiotic along with my bread? So I have named this special manna "penicillin bread." To add to the richness of this breakfast, I also received a piece of marmalade. I still can't decide whether it was made of apples, pears, plums, or straw, for I did find a piece of straw in it. Who knows? The legacy of this never-before-seen marmalade is that to this day, seeing anything in a store by this name will make my hair stand on end.

This was breakfast. I sat there, dumbstruck, and remembered the tantalizing fragrances of the breakfasts my mother used to prepare for me. I almost gave up on eating breakfast at all, when I remembered my father, who had spent four years in Russian prison camps after the war. He survived those horrible years, and here I was, being finicky. I seemed to hear his voice from a great distance. *"Son, it is better than nothing. Close your eyes and fill up your stomach, because dying of starvation is a lot worse than this breakfast."* Whether it was a voice from heaven or my misery that took me close to my father in my thoughts, I don't know. I closed my eyes and finished eating. Good breakfast or bad, what was important was a full belly. Well, maybe not quite full. It wasn't enough for that, but it was something for the mill of the stomach to grind instead of thin air.

After I finished my meal, I thought I would lie on my cell bed and ponder over my worse future. It would have been nice, wouldn't it? It is not what happened, though. The guards herded us outside, like cattle, to the yard, where big trucks were waiting. We prisoners climbed on board of the trucks, to the tune of the guards cursing, and were taken to the workplace.

The workplace was a section of the riverbank outside town. We were to fortify the bank with rocks to protect the town from floods, which were frequent around there. It was beastly, heavy labor to raise the bank with a shovel, move, roll, and fit the rocks in place with an iron bar. The worst part was that if they didn't fit, I had to break them up with a twenty-kilo hammer. Splitting them seemed to break my brain with every blow.

Small bits and pieces of stone were flying mercilessly, hitting my arms, my chest, my face. Sharper slivers cut into my skin like harpoons, drawing blood that mixed with the pouring sweat that was stinging and burning my whole body.

And the time! Oh, God! I didn't know how many hours I had been working, but I could barely stand. I was nauseous, my ears were ringing, and a particularly annoying buzz invaded my brain, which made me feel as if thousands of mosquitoes were flying around in my head.

My arms started to give up also. I felt them weaken after every blow of the hammer. But what could I do? I was crumbling stone and weeping. Weeping not for my pains or my weakness, but for the injustice! I was weeping for freedom!

During work, I kept glancing at the muddy river and thinking of suicide. *Why should I suffer any longer? Why fight the unbeatable? It is simple,* I thought. *I'll throw myself into the river and give my body over to the secretive depth of the yellowish water, which will free me forever.*

My thoughts were almost followed my action when, as if from a great distance, pictures of my dear mother and father appeared—Father with a warning finger and Mother with tears in her eyes. I heard the voice of my father too. *"Son, why do you want to pain us? Don't do anything silly, Son. Suffer a little longer. Now you are suffering, but you will overcome time, and you will win. You will win, Son. You will win."* It kept repeating in my head. The faces of my mother and father disappeared, and I gave up the idea of suicide. *However severely my fate will treat me, I'll fight. I will fight, till fate will give up and leave my battered soul in peace,* I thought.

I broke up the stone. *"You will win, Son. You will win, Son."* Here is another one, a stone! *"You will win, Son."* I was getting dizzy. I'd faint from exhaustion soon. But what was this sound? It was the siren, signaling lunch! I looked up toward the sky, grateful to God, as I collapsed on a boulder.

I did not care how miserable the lunch looked. I just needed to eat—eat to gain strength. The lunch was supposed to be rice curry, but I wondered when the meat had been stolen, for I hadn't seen a piece, not even one the size of a flea. But I was eating the rice greedily, taking huge bites with it from the "penicillin-bread."

Was it hard to swallow? No problem. I helped it down with a mouthful of murky, tepid water. How good these guards were! They would not want the poor prisoners to get pneumonia from drinking ice-cold water. Darn considerate.

Everything started to look up for me. Rice curry without meat, uncooled, murky water, and rest. That rest was valuable beyond belief. I tried to massage my arms, hoping to relieve the pain in my muscles. I would have loved to spread out on my back and sleep till the end of times.

I was just about to try that when I heard the merciless siren again, signaling the end of the lunch break.

After lunch, I returned to my beastly work, though my body ached all over and my palms were full of blisters from the hammer. The dust burned my eyes, and they felt as if they were two flaming furnaces. I knew, however, that no matter what shape I was in, there would not be another break till the sun went down.

I checked on the sun all the time. But the sun seemed to be motionless. It sat in the middle of the sky, as if someone had nailed it there and made it immovable just to torture me. I stopped looking at it. Better to forget sun, the time, and everything. If not, I would have a nervous breakdown by the end of six months or jump into that yellow river for sure.

After all, this was only my first day, and it had not even passed yet. I had to forget everything. I had to break the stone! I needed to slam it hard, as if it were the head of a Communist. Let it crush; let it crumble to pieces. I broke the stone, then fitted it into place with the crowbar, and then broke some more. A flaming inner fury engulfed me. My body was ruled by unknown, raging nerves.

I don't know how long I worked with this inner rage, but suddenly, the siren sounded again, which ended the workday. I looked up at the sky. The sun was gone. Maybe someone had stolen it to shorten the day for us miserable political prisoners.

We returned to the prison, each mate more tired than the next. Tired—we dragged ourselves like wounded animals. We dragged our broken bodies, with our heads hanging low, almost as if they were not part of our bodies and were attached only as an afterthought.

The faces—all the gray, dirty faces—looked exactly the same. I did not see a single smile. Every one of them individually, and all of them combined, showed a total lack of interest in life. They could throw away their broken bodies without much hesitation.

Supper came before we could go into our separate cells. It isn't worth much to describe supper, except maybe to put my readers' worries to rest. We were not forced to go to bed without one. There was supper. To save us from unnecessary excitement, we had the same meal that we ate for lunch: the rice curry, without the meat. (Stolen or not yet born? What difference did it make?) Nobody could be blamed about this in Romania. They voted about these things unanimously. The prisoners should have rice curry. If the cattle for the beef have not been born yet, whose fault is that?

You should not worry too much about these questions, though. It could be harmful for your health. Rice was good enough, with a slice of brown bread and a cup of black coffee. *Enough,* of course, does not imply that I got full. You could call yourself lucky if you didn't get jaundice from disgust.

After this "more than enough" supper, everybody returned to his cell, where he could lose himself in thoughts of a more promising tomorrow. One prisoner entertained the others by bellowing arias from operettas, until the guards had enough and silenced the unknown musician with a few blows to his head. Another prisoner gave a lecture analyzing the similarities between the French and the Romanian language. Somebody else was prophesying about the end of the world, based on his intimate knowledge of the heavenly bodies. Finally, someone simply roared, imitating the sounds of wild animals. I lay on my bed and listened to this chaos and felt that this prison would soon turn into a lunatic asylum.

Oh, God! Would it happen to me too? Would I turn into a half-wit like these poor creatures around me? I wondered what would become my obsession. Would I become Napoleon or maybe the Dalai Lama, or would I start singing operettas, like that other unfortunate soul? Who knew? I was staring into the darkening space with the expression of a half-wit. Idleness had to be the most dangerous enemy.

As I stared at the water trickling down the walls of the cell, I got goose bumps on my back. Suddenly, I leaped from my bed and touched the wet walls. I felt the coldness of ice under my palms. It was cold in the cell too; yet still, I broke out in a sweat. I started to shake with such a force that my teeth were chattering. I started pacing in the narrow cell, rubbing my shivering body. A terrible fear got a hold of me. I was afraid that in the next six months, the cold, wet cell would kill me. This cold dampness is like a leech. It will work its way into your body little by little, day by day, until it reaches the marrow of your bones. Then it will squeeze those bones till your every move becomes torture. There is no way to protect yourself;

the dampness will do its damaging work during the night, while you are asleep. You can't get a hold of it to disarm it. You can't immobilize it, for it has no body. Yet dampness is a very real danger. It will torture you every day, and if it corrupts your body, you will feel its harmful effects for years to come. What could I do? Idleness and the wetness of the cell: these were the two greatest enemies I would have to overcome.

From the left and right of the hallway, deep, hoarse, coughing snores reached me. Some were rapid and rhythmical, while others were continuous, low and rumbling. Still others were regularly interrupted by fits of cough. Without further analysis, I knew that the cause of them all was the wetness of the cells.

I looked at my bed. It must have been painted gray once, for this color still showed through under the rust here and there. It was covered with a horse blanket—the kind that was used to cover horses after a long ride, to protect them from sudden chill. This one, however, had more holes than fabric, and it seemed so old, I was afraid it might disintegrate if I touched it. *I sure can't frolic much under this one,* I thought. One kick, and you would have no more blanket. This should cover someone who was permanently still. *This blanket will not protect me from the wet chill, and within a few days, I will have a new kind of cough, just like my prison mates.*

I started to feel the cold more and more in my limbs. I tried to warm myself with some quick exercises. It helped some, but for what a price! At the movement of every muscle, pain shot through me—the muscle ache, the result of the beastly day's work. I could not keep doing this until the morning, even if it would ward off the cold. I had to rest. I had to lie down to sleep. Otherwise, I would be half dead the next morning, and there certainly would be no mercy here. They would take me to the work site even if I were half-dead. If I died, no big deal. There were enough political prisoners to take my place. Depressed, I sat down on the bed and looked at the mattress. It answered my touch with a rattle. *What the hell?* I thought. *This is science, technology, and civilization!* The mattress was filled with straw. That was the rattling sound. I had just traveled back a hundred years in time. Our great grandfathers used to call this the "straw bag."

I was delighted. This "straw bag" would be my salvation, the protector of my health. It would save me from the cold dampness. I folded away the blanket and made a small hole in the fabric of the mattress with my finger.

Then, slowly, so that wouldn't make any sound, I started to rip open the mattress. The fabric tore easily. When I ripped it the full length, I pushed all the straw to one side, and I lay down. To be exact, I laid into the mattress and covered myself with the straw. The straw smelled moldy, but so what. I pulled the blanket over the straw to cover it. This way, even if the guard looked in on me during the night, he would only see me under the blanket. He would never know I was sleeping in the mattress and not on it. He would only find out if I kicked my blanket off in my sleep, because then he would see me inside the mattress. I didn't have to worry about that too much, though. The guards were too lazy to do much checking on the prisoners' sleep. Rightly so, for there was no chance of anybody escaping, unless they turned into a bodiless substance and slipped out as air through the rusty rails. But how far away is science from the stage when men will be freed from their bodies and shot all over in the universe? Very, very far away! So the lazy guards could sleep peacefully, too, in their grotesque, fat bodies. May their sleep last forever!

I could not fall asleep. I closed my eyes and tried to force sleep. My body was in a good condition indeed. The straw kept me warm. I didn't feel the chill of the cell at all. I felt like a baby bird in a warm nest, under feathers of his mother. I would have liked to shout for joy, but I only wiped a few tears from my eyes instead. How valuable a little moldy straw can be! I had a warm bed for the next six months, which would reduce the chances of my getting pneumonia.

I would have liked to share my discovery of a warm bed with my prison mates, but that was impossible. If everybody followed my example and it was to be discovered, I would lose every last straw. I was protecting my health. No! In prison, everybody has to look out for himself. There, your guiding wisdom is not "help your fellow human beings," but instead, "help yourself." This prison was like a swamp. You were submerged in it up to your neck. You had to try to keep your head out, or you would disappear forever, and there would be no helping hands to pull you up. The secretive black mud would swallow you. Your name would be erased from the list of the living, and you would be forgotten forever. This was prison, full of sinking bodies. Who would win—the bodies or the black mud? Who knew? That was the secret of the future. It was sure, though, that even if the bodies would eventually win, the greedy mud would have swallowed many of them before that.

My secret had to remain my secret, even if it hurt to hear the other prisoners' coughs on the right and left of me. My God, what could I do? I had to fight for my survival! *I have to fight. I have to fight.* It kept repeating in my head, until sleep finally overtook me. Its only offerings, however, were nightmares, so it was not only my body that was to suffer during the beastly work of the day, but also my soul, weighed down under my dreams. The cruel days and torturous nights seemed to be in competition as to which could make me suffer more.

The next morning, the routine started again. Breakfast, the same. Daily work, the same. Supper, the same. Not much sense to even talk about it. Unless the devil took me once during one of my terrible nightmares, for Lucifer visited me regularly, with all his friends and family, to praise the possibilities of hell. How could hell even compare to prison? To any serious inspection, hell must fall short, despite all its scary reputation. I bet prison would come out on top.

Of course, it is also possible that the prison was a department of hell. The guards were Lucifer's executioners, who only acted on his command. The Communists try to keep such things secret. Maybe Ceausescu, the Romanian president, is Lucifer himself, the chief of all devils. These may all sound like jokes, but to whom else could I compare the president and all his Communist cronies? Weren't they herding the people like slaves toward their destiny? There was no smile in this country that would not be phony. You could not hear laughter, unless the one laughing was insane, jesting about his suffering, about the oppression of his rights.

Thought like these were flashing through my mind in the hours of the evening idleness. They were comical at times, outrageous at other times. I was either sinking in self-pity or feeling melancholy. Changes in my mental state came like the sudden flashes of the meteors on the night sky. My mood swings carried me from shrill laughter to deep despair. I knew this was all the result of mental idleness. I was sure this would lead to serious trouble. In six months, I could turn into an operetta singer, or Napoleon, or maybe Romanian President Ceausescu himself, and give speeches about world peace to my fellow prisoners and our guards.

No! Idleness will keep mixing its cards until it deals you a royal flush if you do not take hold of your meandering thoughts. Just you wait, idleness, you are not going to play poker with me, with your marked cards! They were close to being right in the old times, believing that idleness is the devil's workshop. In idleness, your thoughts are wandering aimlessly in the corridors of your mind, until they find the wrong path. Then they will weave their fabric from all that is harmful. When they are done, you are ready for anything: to steal, to rob, to murder. If you are not a criminal, you will surely become insane.

I was wandering those paths! I was drafting plans to beat the police chief to a pulp after my release, or rob his house, or other insane ways to get even. Luckily, I had enough strength to turn my thoughts back, but then they started down the road toward lunacy. This usually gave great pleasure to the guards. They have seemed to particularly enjoy noticing the first signs of craziness in the prisoners. Of course they did, since they had been the ones reinforcing the idleness!

I must have been a lucky one. I have managed to escape from the road to becoming criminal. This caused considerable disappointment to some of my prison mates, who were well advanced in that direction. They viewed me as a new candidate and possible partner in their bright future escapades. I had managed to avoid the road to the murky waters of insanity also. This also disappointed some of my fellow prisoners. The singer, for example, was hoping to perform duets with me, to the greater enjoyment of our mates. The one imitating the animal sounds offered me the role of the zebra. He would roar like a lion, and I could whinny like the cornered zebra, and we could play out the bloody night sounds of the wild. He was considerate enough to assure me that he would not really eat me up; it would all be just pretense. Maybe he wasn't quite insane after all.

The result of this was, though, that I became a loner. I did not belong to any groups. The guards were rather sorry about that. One guard mentioned that he had rather hoped I would join the singer. That would have given him the chance to drum the wake-up calls on my head. He was the same one who wanted to drum on my head the first morning. I wonder what he had against my head? Maybe he had caught some of the lunacy of the place too and imagined himself a drum major?

In the idle even hours, after the hard work of the day, I tried to keep my mind occupied by recreating the details of my aborted attempt to escape the country. I played it in my mind as a silent movie, over and over again. I wanted to find the mistake I had made. My plan to cross the Romanian-Hungarian border was a good one—or so I had thought, in my arrogance—and now I was paying for that mistake. I have learned since to call any plan *sure* only after it has been accomplished fully. Until then, nothing is absolutely reliable. Your own trust in a plan is not enough to make it safe. A plan hatched in your mind seems easy. The test of it, though, is the reality of time and place—when you are on location, the seconds start rolling, and you discover all the incidental unplanned events that you will have to negotiate into your design.

It is rather safe to bet that you can cross the street safely when the light is green. Still, you can wake up from your daydreams to the screeching of brakes and find yourself under a vehicle that couldn't stop in time. You lose your bet.

This is what happened to me. My plan was perfect, theoretically, so I made a bet with myself. Then the reality of place and time scrambled my design, and I lost because I had not given consideration to the incidentals of place and time.

So let the film roll, the silent movie of my attempt to escape through the Romanian-Hungarian border. I was not far from the actual border. I had arrived there by train. I got off in a little village, the last one before ID checks are required on the train by the border guards. I didn't loiter in the village; I tried to leave its boundaries as soon as I could. The fewer people saw me there, the better. In a little village like this, everybody knows everybody else, and 90 percent of the population is made up of informants to the border patrol. A stranger in a small place like this close to the border is noticeable, like an elephant among sheep. Even if I didn't have to worry about snitches in the village, I couldn't stay there long. The law requires that in every village or town near the border, a visitor must register with the local police and produce his picture ID and other personal papers. The police then check out his reasons to visit the area. He may come to see relatives or inquire about work, but he has to prove it and state the length of time he wants to spend there. They double-check everything before giving him the permit to stay. There are no chances of getting away with a lie. If they find anything suspicious, they simply arrest him and keep him for further investigations.

The Communists had organized this quite efficiently to make sure nobody had the slightest chance to escape from that glorious place of theirs.

I had no other alternatives but to disappear from the vicinity of the village as fast as I could, lest I be forced to wrestle with the perplexities of the law. I approached the border in concealment of the woods. During the day, I tried to find cover and sleep, or at least rest. When darkness came, I left my hiding place and continued my exhausting trip. The night was dark, and only distant lightning flashed occasionally. A storm was coming. A strong wind was blowing toward me, pushing the storm before it. The storm was coming fast. The rumbling sound accompanying the flashes of the lightning was getting louder by the minute. It was an eerie night. I bumped into bushes, stumbled and fell, and then got up, only to be dragged down again by thorns, as if they were the invisible hands of ghosts. I freed myself from the brambles and then staggered on in the darkness, when suddenly, someone slapped me across the face. At least, that's what I thought at first. Thank God, it was only a low branch snapping back. My lips were cut, but what did that matter? It's infinitely better to be slapped by a tree than by a human. The rumbling sound now changed into deafening blows, and rain started to pour as if all the faucets were opened full-force up there.

I got soaked in a matter of seconds, but I could not stop. If the end of the world were nearing, I still could not have stopped. I had to go on. Whether to crawl or slither in the mud, be ripped by thorns or slapped by branches, I could not stop. Lightning was flashing across the sky right above me, but I had to go on. Time was passing, swallowing up the minutes fast, taking big bites of the night. And I needed time. I had to have time, for when I got close to the border, in the last kilometer, I couldn't afford to bump into bushes or to trip over dead branches anymore. I couldn't create the slightest noise there. This last kilometer was the last and greatest test—the "sevenfold trial" of fairy tales, when one had to approach the castle of the princess and fight his way through dragons, witches, and all sorts of creepy-crawly monsters. But how easy it is in the fairy tales. The prince always conquers the dangers and wins the love of the beautiful princess, and they live happily ever after.

That was the fairy tale. My last kilometer, however, was full of real-life dangers. The most dangerous things were the signaling rockets. They were hidden by the thousands and connected with thin wires that crisscrossed the whole area like a tight web. The wires were covered by fallen leaves, hidden in the grass, and topped by sand. I knew about them, so I tried to be extremely careful. If my shoe were to get tangled in those devilish wires, several of the rockets would fire up, and whistling sound and bright-orange flares would light up the night around me. There was no escape after that. In a matter of seconds, the border guards would get me—unless one over-anxious guard sent a bullet into me right then and there. And do you think he would get reprimanded for that? He would get a week's vacation and a medal of honor for his patriotic heroism. With laws like that, I would not have been surprised if they were to simply shoot me instead of capturing me.

The rain slowly subsided; the stores up in the sky seemed to have run out. The moon was hiding in and out of the torn clouds. This was bad, for if it came out completely, the night would be a lot lighter, and I would become more visible. I neared the edge of the woods. The light of strong reflectors was seeping in among the last trees. About five meters from the edge of the woods, I stopped and sat down on a log to rest. Here I was, in torn clothes bleeding from the cuts, muddy and wet, with the last kilometer in front of me—the dangers of the final sevenfold trial. But as the prince in the fairy tales always wins his prize, the beautiful fairy princess, would I win my prize? Would my lucky star guide me? Or was I only a meteor, shining brightly for a short time and falling into a final defeat?

Lucky star or meteor, these were nice thoughts, but I couldn't play with them right then. I couldn't play "heads or tails" or "to go or not to go." I had no way back anymore, and even if I had, I would not have wanted it, for turning back would mean the unfair, tortuous, humiliating oppression. The road to the castle of my fairy princess—my freedom—was ahead of me!

I got up from the log and walked to the very edge of the woods. Silence and darkness. I did not have to worry about the floodlights yet. They were still far away, the darkness swallowed up their beams. I had to watch out for the warning rockets. I moved slowly, with infinite care. Instead of the usual back-and-forth motions, I lifted my foot straight up, robot-like, at every step, and put it down again straight and gentle. This robot walk was slow, but safe. This way, if I stepped on a wire, it would lay flat under my sole instead of getting tangled up by my shoes. I felt my heartbeat in my throat, as if my heart was trying to escape my body by moving higher and higher up until it could leap out through the nape of my neck. It seemed as if my heart was protesting the decision of my mind and body about this flight. Maybe my heart was just not strong enough to match my body and my mind. It is possible. After all, my heart is not made of stone. Sometimes I wished it was, and then I would not feel its beating in my throat and my ears constantly, like the drumroll of an executing brigade. But I am human, after all, not a robot—a human, like the billions and billions of others on this earth. I felt, saw, heard, smelled, cried, or laughed, as conditions dictated, like all the other human beings. I was the same way as they were. No more, no less. I felt pain cutting my fingers. And now, my heart was beating unbearably in my throat, because I wanted to escape. I wanted my human right, which had been stripped off me to the point of making me feel utterly naked. I was naked and lonely on a field planted with warning rockets.

I continued my slow advance, never forgetting the unnatural, robot-like steps. I looked back toward the woods, but I could not make them out anymore. They had blended into the darkness. In front of me, as I was getting closer to the floodlights, the winding outline of some shrubs started to show in the dimness. *That must be the river,* I thought, I and turned toward it, still keeping the careful, gentle steps, for I was still in the cursed fields of the rockets. Finally, I reached the bushes. I was right! I could now hear the murmur of the water. I slowly descended to the bank, behind the bushes. It would be best to swim across the river, for it seemed there were fewer floodlights on the other side. I am not a good swimmer, though, so I stayed away from the river. I might have tried it, if we haven't had a rainy few weeks recently, but as it was unusually high, running wildly with boiling torrents, it would have been a challenge even for an expert.

I stayed on this side of the river and sat down. I unpacked my food, for my stomach was protesting loudly. While I had a quick bite, I lay on my stomach and studied my map. Good thing I had packed everything in plastic bags, so they stayed dry. I buried my head under my coat before I turned my flashlight on to look at the map. As I looked at the map, I rejoiced that I had decided against swimming. Had I done that, I would have had a route that was about three times longer than on this side, because of the winding river. In the cover of the bushes hugging the bank of the river on this side, I would be able to approach the floodlights undetected. Not far from my position, the map showed a fairly large bend in the river. That is where I was going to depart from it and turn straight toward the Romanian border.

I packed everything away in my backpack, except my binoculars and the mixture of alcohol and formaldehyde. I quickly undressed and rubbed my whole body with this mix, then put my clothes back on before my body dried so that my clothes would soak up the moisture from my skin. I used this mix to throw the German shepherds off scent. They have extremely accurate scent and are trained to sniff out humans. Once they caught your scent, there was no escape. You were better off not even trying, for they would knock you down and tear you to pieces before their master even got there. Of course, he would be in no hurry to rescue you.

I double-checked everything. I gave my backpack a couple of good shakes to make sure nothing inside would rattle or make any noise. It seemed safe and silent. I hung my binoculars on my neck and then buttoned my coat over them. Everything was in order. I got up and started to walk. The wind was cutting strongly in my face. It was blowing toward me! Oh, God, how good you are to me! This gave the dogs even less of a chance to catch my scent.

It didn't take long to reach the bend of the river. I was surprised at how easy it was. I pulled out my binoculars and, hiding behind a bush, searched for the border guards. When I found them, I tried to follow their every move. I explored the area I would have to cross. I noted the area each guard patrolled and the length of the time it took him to make a round. I checked the point where they met and measured the time that lapsed between the two meetings. Ten minutes—not great, but not too bad either. I had ten minutes while after their meetings, the two guards would turn their backs to each other and walk the opposite direction. Meeting their partners on the other side, they would turn again and walk the other way.

They continued this pacing up and down until the time came to change guards at the end of their shift. This was my puzzle to be solved. Adding to the challenge were the officers with the dogs, who periodically checked on the guards. It was not going to be easy, but I had to finish what I had started. I never liked to abandon any task once I started it.

Determined, I waited for the guards to meet, and then I started moving as soon as they turned their backs to each other. I moved in a tiring crawl. It was very slow-going. I had crossed less than a quarter of the distance when I had to stop and lie flat down on the grass, because the guards were already on their way back toward each other. It felt good to lie in the grass, for I needed the rest. The grass was tall, tall enough so I could not be seen laying in it. Even the grass, with its lush growth, was helping me. It protected me as it covered me from evil eyes.

The guards met, turned around, and started their walk again. I started my silent crawl too, a snake-like slither, and then I rested, lying in the grass. Again and again, this continued until I got close to the guard towers. Four towers were particularly dangerous: the four equipped with the floodlights, aiming in opposite directions. A guard stood in every tower with binoculars and a long-range shotgun. With the floodlights, they made wide, sweeping motions left and right to illuminate vast half-circles of the field. The bright strands of light were moving in regular intervals across my path. I was at the Romanian border, separated from freedom by these last fifty meters! Fifty meters! But the floodlights seemed to make these last fifty meters impossible to cross. How could anybody pass through here, unless he became bodiless and swept through like the wind? I felt desperate. My chances of getting through suddenly seemed closer to zero than to one. I became more and more nervous, too, as the night wore on and morning was forthcoming. I had no time. I had to decide and act—to go ahead, or to back down. Unfortunately, I didn't have a real choice. I could only go ahead. Turning back at this point would have meant more trouble, even figuring nothing but the time element. If I went back now, the morning light would find me in the field of the warning rockets!

Trying to calm myself, I started to do the only thing I could do. I started to study the movements of the floodlights. Luck seemed to be with me again! I noticed that the light coming from the fourth tower was not as strong as the others. This left a little area less illuminated than the rest of the field. This strip looked like a narrow hallway in a cellar. Its opening was dimly lit, but its length was impossible to gauge, for it disappeared into dusk. At least, this was the picture that came into my mind about this half-lit passage. I also noticed that this guard was not particularly interested in what was happening down there. He was moving the reflector left and right with his hand, but his eyes were occupied by something else. I could not make out what it was he was holding in his other hand, but whatever it was, he was reading it. The poor idiot. If an officer were to catch him, he would be done in. You were not allowed a cigarette while on guard duty, never mind reading! Yet, this guard was reading! Reading and smiling, as if he were in a waiting room somewhere, not on guard duty.

Well, idiotic or not, that was *his* problem. What was important to me was that this gave me a chance. Maybe he was reading a love letter. What do rules matter when you are in love? May God make all the border guards fall in love. How easy that would make life for me! Chances of this happening were not much better than winning the lottery, so I left it at that. I checked over all the towers and their guards once again. Satisfied that everything was as before, I started for the last fifty meters. I crawled slowly in the tall grass, leaving meter after meter behind me. I started to feel warm all over inside, almost within reach of freedom. I was in line of the tower already. That meant I had done twenty-five meters already. Another twenty-five to go—a little more, just a little more. I was dead tired. My arms were quivering from exhaustion, but I didn't stop. *Go on; go on,* I told myself.

Maybe this self-assurance was my downfall. There is no sense looking for the reason. It had happened, and nothing could change it anymore. You can't escape your destiny. Whoever guided mine would not let me go any further. *"This far, human, and no more! I am your fate in good times and in bad. If I want it, I play tricks on you. I can make you cry if I feel like it, give you luck or shower you with troubles. You little worm. You have no power against my will. I rule everywhere in your past and in your future, accompanying you throughout your life."*

I mention destiny, for mine was to lose here. I only needed to crawl fifteen more meters to reach my freedom. But I never saw the end of those fifteen meters. A bird took off in front of me from the tall grass. Maybe a pheasant. He broke the silence of the night with his scared, loud, crackling sound. In the distance behind me, I heard the barking of the German shepherds. I laid low in the grass, listening. I knew one of the guards must have noticed the bird taking off and gotten suspicious. He had let the dogs loose to check out his hunch. If there was nothing, the dogs would come back. But I had no illusions about that. I was there, and the dogs would find me. I tried to change direction, but I didn't get far before I reached the beam of the reflectors. I was in a trap. This was the end, but what kind of end, I had no way of knowing. I thought I would jump up to my feet and run like hell. But I abandoned this thought as fast as it came. The guards would shoot me in the back, or the dogs would reach me first and tear me to pieces, or if neither happened, I would run into the Hungarian border guards. Though it might've pained them to surrender me, a fellow Hungarian, to the Romanian border patrol, they would not have had a choice but to do just that. That was the law—the pact between two Communist countries.

I was still hoping. *Maybe the dogs won't notice me after all.* But this hope soon departed too. The barks were getting closer. Finally, it had happened. Hunting for a bird, they had found a human. When they found me, they started to bark hysterically. I didn't move. I knew that was the signal they were awaiting for so they could sink their teeth into me. Only my heart was beating, so wildly it was as if it wanted to burst out of my chest. The circle of the dogs was getting tighter and tighter around me. They were barking and growling, watching me for the slightest move. This didn't last long, though, before the shapes of the guards started to materialize from the darkness. They came with their guns aimed at me, ready to release their ammo into my body, should I make a suspicious move. I didn't dare to breathe. Then an officer left the group with a flashlight in his hand. He crouched down next to me and shone the light into my face. His handgun was in his other hand, and he pressed it against my temple. I felt the coldness of the metal, and thought, *My God, this is the end. Let it come fast.* But it didn't come fast. The officer made sure I suffered some first. All the minutes while he entertained himself were giving me gray hair. He started to talk me.

"What happened? Did you get lost?"

I did not answer.

"I think you have tried to escape, you maggot."

18

Again, I didn't answer.

"Well, this idiot can't talk. Don't worry, we will teach you how to talk. Matter of fact, you will even sing." He pulled the trigger. The gun was empty.

"Now, look at that; I thought the gun was loaded," he said as he stood up.

"Okay, get up," he ordered. "Handcuff this beast, and escort him in. I don't like slow people." He kicked my ribs before I could get up.

I clambered onto my feet painfully, and the procession took off: me, as a political prisoner, they, as the protection bastions of Communism.

I dissipated. Everything disappeared like smoke. The dreams of countless nights, the plans of endless days, the miserable trials and tests, ended in one second. Nobody can tell me a bird cannot be the end of you. I know it can. A snake, a skunk, even a grasshopper can bring you down, if they are where you are and where they are not supposed to be. You jump up, startled by a snake, and you are found. You come across a skunk, start coughing from its stink, and you are found. A grasshopper gets into your clothes, you itch yourself, and you are found. The list could go on forever. Everything is against you when you are trying to crawl noiselessly. Who would ever have guessed that a pheasant would become my snitch? I surely would have laughed at the idea.

You have to learn from your own mistakes. I had certainly made a promise to myself, that if I ever got out of this alive, I would never discount the unexpected effects of the animal world on my plans. This may sound funny from a distance, but since a pheasant caused my downfall, I don't ever want to see them again, not even as roasts on my table.

The guards were taking me into a grayish, dilapidated building. They shoved me into a small interrogating room and locked the iron door behind me. I looked around. There wasn't much to see: a wooden table and two wooden chairs, that was all for furniture. Nothing hanging on the walls. Actually, what was even stranger was that the walls and ceiling were all painted red. Standing in the middle of the room, I was wondering, why on earth did they paint everything red? I found out later, of course.

I was about to sit down when I heard footsteps from the hallway, and the iron door opened with a loud squeak. First, a tall, fat, pig-faced commander entered the room, followed by the officer and guard who had captured me. The officer put some papers on the table, then remained standing behind it. The guard closed the iron door and stood in front of it, motionless, as if he were nailed there. The commander sat down. The chair was protesting against his great weight so loudly that I thought it would collapse any minute. But it held. He lit a cigarette and smoked it without a word for a long time. He took pleasure from checking me out from head to toe, slowly, thoroughly, with a sarcastic smirk on his face. I could feel it in my gut, that I was facing a hard-core, true believer of Communism, who was set on tearing me to shreds. These idle moments had sent ants into the souls of my feet, biting and crawling. Finally, after what seemed an eternity, the commander addressed me in a gentle tone.

"Sit down, son. Take a cigarette if you smoke, and write down everything. Why did you want to escape from Romania? Don't forget the names of those who helped you. In other words, write down everything, son. I mean everything."

I knew what the pig face wanted. He wanted a signed confession that they could use against me in court. That way, I would get a minimum five-year sentence immediately. However, I wasn't a total idiot. I pretended, though, that I was. I accepted the cigarette, lit it, and sat down. To secure some time to enjoy the cigarette, I slowly pulled the papers in front of me and feigned total absorption in the recent events. I finished smoking the cigarette while the pig face with bloodshot eyes was waiting for me to start writing my confession. He was looking forward to getting a promotion from this, as a reward for his true patriotism. He could improve his great body and expressive facial features, as I whiled away the next five years in prison. What did five years of my youth mean to him? Not much. He had probably sent scores of others to the slammer to get yet another star on his shoulder.

He must have gotten tired of waiting, for he started up again.

"Well, son, get started." That's where the first bomb exploded, for I looked up at him, dumb and innocent.

"Start what, Comrade Commander?" I asked.

"Start what?" he repeated my question. "Well, start writing your confession about the details of your plan to escape."

"There must be some mistake here, commander," I said. "I didn't want to escape." And here came the second bomb: as I was lifting the cigarette to my lips, I received such a blow across my face that the cigarette stub flew across the room.

By now, his gentle voice had changed too. He lunged at me with a roar, grabbed me by my jacket, and yanked me up from the chair. He shook me as if I were a fruit tree and hollered into my face from so close that his spit showered my whole face.

"You moron, you idiotic jerk, you lowlife of a traitor. Are you playing a game with me? Just you wait, you insolent crap. You will get to know me soon enough." With that, he pushed me away with such a force that I fell on my ass.

"Get up, you little shit, and I recommend that you start writing real fast this time."

Before I had time to get up, though, the officer kicked me with his heavy boots. As I was scrambling to my feet, his kick got me right in my gut. The sharp pain almost took my breath away.

"Get moving, you maggot!" he yelled at me. "Or do you need another kick in your belly to speed you up? You'll get it, believe me, if you don't do what the Comrade Commander wants you to do."

I dragged myself to the table with tight lips, lest I would say something offensive about their mothers, which I was sure would not have improved my situation. I made up my mind not to write that confession, even if they killed me right there. I would be singing my own sentence. Even this beating was better than five years in prison. So I sat there without a word. But not for long, for the commander slammed his fist at the table, so the papers were flying all over.

"Start writing, you idiot, or I will have you beaten to death."

"There is nothing for me to confess," I said timidly. "I came to this area as a hiker. I got lost at night, and when I realized where I was, I tried to hide in the tall grass, because I was afraid it would be trouble if I were found out. And of course, I was right, for now I am accused unfairly." This sounded like a smart speech, but the commander was no fool. He let out a sinister laugh.

"So you are a hiker, and you got lost?" he said, laughing wildly. "Then why was your backpack full of maps, a compass, tools, and binoculars? I tell you why, you wicked jerk. Because you wanted to escape from Romania. I know the likes of you. I have met a few pimps like you before, and they still remember me in their dreams. Do you understand? They still remember me. You better start writing, or you will remember me and this day till the end of your life. You'll pass down my memory even to your great-grandchildren, that is, if you get out of my hands alive." He stopped his tirade and waited for my reaction.

The whole inside of my body was trembling from fear, for I knew if I said no, all this treatment would appear as tenderness compared to what was to come. But five years! I would throw away five years, when everything was pointing against me as it was. No, I could not do that. I had to continue to deny everything.

"There is nothing for me to confess, or write, Comrade Commander," I insisted. "As I said earlier, I am a hiker. Everything you had found in my backpack, I need for my hikes."

The commander leaped from his seat and yelled in a nervous voice.

"Enough of this garbage. You will get your real lesson." He turned to the soldier standing guard by the door.

"Give this jerk his lesson," he ordered. Nervously, he motioned to the officer, and both of them left the room, followed by a loud bang of the door.

The soldier knew what was expected of him. Acting like a robot, without saying or asking a word, he started to beat me with both fists, anywhere he could reach me. I felt the blood spurt out of my nose. My lips were cut, and my stomach tightened into a knot. I fell on the floor. This didn't help either. As I lay there doubled over, the damn soldier started to use his boots, kicking me like a soccer ball. This was worse than his fists.

I can't tell you how long he worked on me, for I lost consciousness. When I came to, I realized I was alone in the room. I tried to stand up, but I had no strength. I fell back. My ears were buzzing, and I felt that my head had been grilled by a hot iron. I pulled my hand over my head. Unbearable pain answered my touch, and I felt several bumps the size of walnuts. I felt a sticky, slippery wetness on my fingers. Looking at my hands, I saw blood. There was no mirror in the room in which to see my face, but judging from the pain on my skin and in my bones, I had gotten a good "workout." The worst sensation was that I could not breathe through my nose. My nostrils were all clogged up by the dried blood. I tried to pry blood clots loose, but it was too painful, so I soon gave up. The inside of my mouth was burning, as if after tasting a hot pepper, and I could feel a couple of loose teeth as I ran my tongue around in my mouth. My whole body was covered with bruises and bumps turning black and blue. I was out.

I cringed into a small heap on the floor and my eyes filled up with tears—tears gathered not only from the physical pain, but also from the injustice. My thoughts brought back the words of the commander about remembering this day. He was right. For the rest of my life, I would remember the days I spent with him. I was furious about my helplessness. I thought of how in my homeland, human rights were trampled and people were treated like animals. *Who has given them rights to do this? They feel omnipotent. They can stop free-thinking people from doing anything against their Communist system, because they aren't scrupulous about using the most cruel methods. And they do this so that they can continue to steal the poor, exploited pariah blind. The peoples of Romania are treated as dogs. They are told, "Hush, don't you bark, or I hit you on the nose." And the wretched things are silent, for they are afraid. Afraid of the secret police, who can hear them even if they bark behind locked doors.*

How long will they keep quiet, though? How long? The day will come when the people will cry out "Enough" in unison; the word will travel through all the cities, and like a tornado, it will run to the farthest corners of the country. There won't be a living person who can escape hearing this word: enough. *The revolution of the people will then burst open for justice and for freedom. This revolution will crush Communism and break open the chains of slaves, and the "dog's" life will become human life again.*

Distant steps from the hallway outside woke me from my thoughts. I wiped the tears from my eyes, which were brought there by the joyous thoughts of freedom. The steps were nearing the room, and I tried to shrink as small as I could for fear of further beating.

The door opened up, and the commander, the soldier who nearly beat me to death, and three other officers entered. The commander came up to me and walked around me, investigating, as if I were some curious object.

He seemed satisfied with the work of the soldier, for after thorough checking, punctuated with grunts, he finally said, "Get up." With great pain, I pulled myself up by the corner walls. I stood facing him, feeling I would collapse again any minute. I decided I was not going to answer, no matter what he said.

"Now, you see, son," he started, in his gentle voice again. "This is what happens to dirty liars like you. Now, wouldn't it have been better to admit your intention to escape and write that confession? Of course it would have. Everything would have happened differently. You could have had a good meal, a cigarette, and a bed to recover from your adventure. And us? Of course we would have compassion toward you, seeing that you had shown remorse for the sins you had committed against your homeland.

"But you chose not to do this, son. You stubbornly deny everything and try to fool us by silly lies. I hope you have realized this is impossible. You were wrong. I hope your mind is clearing up, or else tomorrow, you will see the next step in your education. Now, son, I leave you here until tomorrow, without any further treatment, so you can see how good I am to you, even though you don't deserve my goodwill. Of course, you won't get any food or water, because you were lying, but you have some time to think it over. You are in a losing position, trying to oppose the blessed laws of this country.

"I hope you understand me, son, and tomorrow, you will write that confession. For if not, you will curse the day you were born."

He finished his long speech, and with the phony sweetness in his voice, he turned to his comrades.

"We can leave now, comrades." They were silent throughout the whole scene, and now they all left with straight backs and upheld heads as the embodiment of Communist morals.

I was happy, if I can use this word, after what happened to me. I was happy because I was alone and had escaped another beating. I knew he was kind to me for a good reason. He figured he might get the damn confession out of me easier this way than with the beating. Without food and water, I would walk into his trap sooner or later. Tomorrow, if I were a good boy, I would get everything. He wasn't such a bad businessman, after all. Five years' imprisonment for the price of a little water and some bread. Well, he could have his bread and water. I would try to save myself the five years. Time was the most important element of the deal, though. I needed time, and I got time. I knew what they didn't think I knew, that the border patrol could not hold anybody longer than forty-eight hours. Whether I confessed or not, after forty-eight hours, they would have to transfer me to the secret military police. This, of course, doesn't mean that in there, my torture would be over and they would treat me with gloved hands. Actually, from the hearsay, I knew that they were the very devils. They said that whoever got into their hands wouldn't come out alive, or if they did come out alive, they'd be insane.

But all this seemed so far away now. All kind of things could happen till then. What was here and now, though, was the fright the commander had awakened in me. I knew him well, after only a short time, and had no hopes for mercy from him. He was a full-blooded Communist who also hated Hungarians. Hate glowed in his eyes. The expression on his face was easy to read: *"Just you wait, you dirty little Hungarian. I will teach you how to appreciate Romania."*

I tried to disconnect my thoughts from the commander and the monstrosities he represented. I couldn't. It was as if his reduced clone had moved into my head.

My body ached all over. I moaned at every motion from the pain, but exhaustion finally took over and I fell asleep on the floor.

When I woke up in the morning, I looked around and said, "Where am I?" Then reality hit me. *I was caught by the border patrol.* The pain in my body was more intense than it had been the day before. The red marks of the beatings started to turn black and blue. I didn't know what time it was or how many hours I had slept, for they had taken my watch. The little room did not have any windows, so I couldn't estimate the time from the sun, either. Why I was even concerned about time, I am not quite sure, since I was not going to go for a morning walk or make plans on how to spend the coming hours. Measuring time for me became the most coveted treasure, simply because there was no way to achieve it. I laughed bitterly about it. Maybe I was simply waiting for my breakfast. And for my lunch and dinner at the same time, for I was so hungry, I could have finished a whole day's meals at once. I suspected, of course, that there wouldn't be any meals coming my way real soon, since they were trying to use my hunger and thirst to break my resistance.

I really had nothing else to do but wait for my kind Communist company to arrive.

I didn't have to wait long. I heard approaching steps, and then the door opened and the pig-faced general appeared, with the glow of a good breakfast on his face. He was accompanied by a different soldier, this time a sergeant. He had a mean, ready-to-kill expression on his face, and he made me more scared than the previous one.

The commander, as was his custom, sat down comfortably and lit a cigarette. This time, he didn't offer me one. I guess I didn't prove worthy. To further harass me, he had a cup of coffee and some pastries ordered for himself. He started to slurp his coffee in a loud, disgusting way, as if a pig were eating from the trough.

The sergeant stood quietly and carefully examined me with his eyes. I noticed something like pity in his eyes, despite the cruel expression on his face. The pity must have been directed to me. I doubt that he felt sorry for the commander, gaining weight by the day. Maybe I reminded him of someone close to his heart who had gotten into trouble before. Or maybe, simply, the gentleness of his human nature came over him and he couldn't escape from feeling sorry about my plight.

The commander finally spoke.

"Well, son, I hope you slept well and thought over your situation wisely. You know what I want. I want you to write that confession. I want to hand you over to the secret military police as meek and obedient as a lamb. Believe me, son, that would be best. If you do not break down here with me, they'll break you there, along with all the bones in your body." Hats off for them! They really knew how to do their jobs.

He was a sly fox, this commander, and a vicious wolf at the same time. He wanted to hang those five years on me the worst way.

Well, you pig-face, I thought, *you won't eat the cream of that one. I am not going to be instrumental in your promotion, so that you can parade around free and well fed, while I rot away in jail for five years. Let death come first.*

"Here are the papers, son. Go ahead; get started."

"Let it be, then," I said calmly and sat down. I pulled the papers in front of me.

Seeing this, the commander's eyes lit up.

"This is it, son," he said to himself. "I knew we would understand each other after yesterday's lesson. Here is a cigarette."

Hunger and thirst were torturing me more. As if the commander could read my mind, he rubbed his hands together and continued.

"Don't worry, son, as soon as you are done with this document, which is important to the state, not to me, anyway (*Sure, sure, you lying pig,* I thought), you will get plenty of food and coffee and cigarettes."

While the commander colored his fancy pictures of lies, I happened to glance at the sergeant. He seemed to look at me with indescribable distaste. I knew I was reading this right, for his whole expression was of disgust, disappointment, and spite.

His eyes seemed to say, *"You poor, misguided idiot, you are digging your own grave! You have given up the fight; you have broken down like a cowardly dog who deserves his lot."* This was, of course, the way I had interpreted his expression. But I knew I was right. I could read faces well.

Don't worry, my friend, I thought. *You'll see how well you judged me.* Hiding a little sarcastic smile, I started to write.

Despite the cruel handling by Comrade Commander, breaking the common law of humane treatment, using methods of the Gestapo, to coerce a confession of a crime I did not commit, I state in writing what I said yesterday in spoken words, that I am an innocent hiker. I got lost near the border and got unintentionally into the forbidden border area. Please, consider my innocence, and realize that I am a victim of some misunderstanding.

Then I couldn't resist putting a saucy closing.

With deepest respect, your faithful compatriot of the Romanian Socialist Republic: Paul D.

Some confession, I thought as I read it over.

"I am finished with my confession, Comrade Commander," I said.

"This fast?" He sounded surprised.

"I didn't have much to write, Comrade Commander. I could only write what had happened."

"You are right, son," he agreed. "Sergeant, read the confession out loud, so that we can all sign it legally."

Well, I thought, *here comes the big bomb!*

The sergeant took the paper, but it seemed as if he had frozen into a stone statue before he could start to read out loud. He stood, motionless, scared stiff.

Dead silence filled the room. The sergeant kept looking at me, then at the commander. The commander didn't know what to make of his silence, so he ordered him again, firmly.

"Read, Sergeant. Didn't you hear my command?"

"But … but … a, a … How can I say this? There is nothing for me to read, Comrade Commander," the sergeant stammered with fright.

"What do you mean, there is nothing to read?" the commander yelled. "Read what is on the paper."

The sergeant continued his stammer. "Well … a, a … what it says … a, a … What is on this paper is that he says he is innocent. He says he didn't try to escape; he is only an innocent hiker."

Hearing this, the commander burst into such a bellow, the walls seemed to shake.

"Show me that paper! All the devils of hell, let me see!" He tore the paper form the hands of the sergeant. His eyes nearly popped from his head as he looked at the paper. There were a few minutes of total silence in the room—the silence preceding the explosion of a most horrendous storm. Even the sergeant stepped back timidly. I seemed to notice an encouraging smile in the corner of his mouth, meant for me as a reward for my guts. It was a short-lived smile, though, for the storm broke out of the commander.

He ran toward me with wide-open mouth, so for a second, I was afraid he was going to bite me. I have never in my life seen a man go so totally wild. He looked like a rabid animal. Even his mouth was foaming.

"You runt, you rat, you maggot!" he screamed. He grabbed my hair with one hand and started to slap me with the other, from the left, then from the right, then left again. I felt as if my head was a tennis ball.

"Did you think we were playing a crossword puzzle here?" he kept hollering. "Just you wait, you little shit; you will get your damn lesson yet. You'll get it, so you will beg me to accept your damn confession." With that, he pushed me away, except that he forgot to let my hair go, so as I fell to the floor, I left a fistful of hair in his hand. As I landed on my ass, I was fully prepared to be his soccer ball next. I expected him to kick me around with his good, sturdy boots, but he didn't. He seemed to have forgotten how to have fun. Instead, he started to pace nervously up and down in the narrow room. Maybe he was wracking his brain about what to do with me next. After a lengthy, scary silence, he called to the sergeant.

"Comrade Sergeant, take care of this idiot and beat some sense into him. The beast would deserve to be shot to death," he yelled irately and then stormed out, leaving me with the sergeant.

After the commander left, I looked at the sergeant timidly, expecting him to continue the job his boss left unfinished. Long minutes had passed, however, and no blows and no kicks came. What would come of this? Finally, the sergeant moved and took a few steps toward me. *Here it comes,* I thought, but I was wrong. He was not coming toward me; he went to the door. He opened it carefully and peeked out. Dumbfounded, I followed his moves with my eyes. Finally, he closed the door and stepped to me. He put his hands on my shoulders. I looked up at him with wearied eyes.

"Listen to me, my friend," he said in a whisper. "I hope you know that I am supposed to be beating you to a pulp right now." I nodded my head in surprise. He continued. "I won't do it, though, because I can see that you already got your share from the other monster. But I don't want to get myself into trouble either. I hope you understand that, too." I nodded my head again. "Good, then you'll only get a few blows from me when I hear the commander's footsteps from the hallway. You can take those. This will save you from the major beating, but it will save me too, from the suspicion of collaboration. Do you understand what I am saying, my friend?"

"Yes, I understand, and I am very grateful," I whispered.

"Don't mention it; it's just human decency. I hope God will forgive me for the beating I will have to give you, knowing that you really are innocent." He spoke in a sad tone of voice and then stood close to the door, so he could hear better when the commander would be coming down the hallway.

Minutes went by, and we waited in silence. He was listening for the footsteps of the commander, and I was watching his face, touched by his nobility.

He is risking his own skin for me, I thought. In the Romanian Army, disobeying an order is equal to treason. He could easily get ten years in a military prison if they found out he had disobeyed. His eyes showed, though, that he was not afraid. He, the simple sergeant, proved that he dared to resist his superior. A commander. He showed that he didn't believe in the unjust methods used by him. He showed that human dignity and compassion are invaluable treasures, and everywhere, there are people willing to protect them. Here, this sergeant was the protector of human rights against gross injustice.

In my heart, I feel he is not the only one in Romania ready to protect human rights. Millions and millions of people feel the same way as this sergeant. They want to protect human rights. They want to stop corruption. They want to allow people to think and move freely. When all this becomes reality, then I, too, will believe that the people freely and voluntarily praise Communism, and not from fear, under duress of pain. Then I will believe that nobody will spit at the sound of the word *Communism*. But this is all the country of dreams, hidden somewhere in the unknown future.

The present was this Communism, and the reality of this Communism was the sergeant and me waiting here. For him, I could only say a quick prayer asking God to protect him from the traitors, so he wouldn't get hurt for what he had done for me.

I was awakened from my warm and fuzzy thought by the noise of steps from outside. The sergeant stepped to me.

"When the door opens, pretend that you are passed out," he whispered. "Understand?"

I had no time to say anything, for he had changed his voice, and he started screaming.

"You worthless slime, you pile of garbage! How long do I have to keep beating on you?"

He gave me a few quick raps, hitting me where I was already wounded anyway. This was a good idea, because he got fresh blood without having to hit too hard. He put on a continuous show for the approaching commander.

"How did you dare contradict the Comrade Commander, you traitor? I'll push your eyes out so you won't ever see the daylight again!"

At this point, the door opened. The sergeant struck me a few more times, so the commander could see it. He saw it and mumbled something approvingly. I pretended to be unconscious.

"Comrade commander, I am not making headway with this animal. I beat him till he fainted but still he kept on saying he is innocent, only a hiker lost who got into the border area by accident."

"I knew he wouldn't admit anything," agreed the commander. "You didn't have to overdo it, though. What if the idiot died on us?"

"I only followed your order, Comrade Commander."

"All right, very well."

I heard him sit down comfortably. The chair squeaked out in pain. He lit a cigarette. I heard the click of the lighter. He sat there, smoking and quietly grunting occasionally like a satisfied groundhog. Why did he sound so content? He should be screaming in frustration after this unsuccessful interrogation. He must have cooked up something really big and new for my future torture.

"How can we untie the tongue of this jerk, Comrade Commander?" asked the sergeant.

"Nothing for the time being," chuckled the commander. "Nothing at all, until this animal wakes up," he continued, as if talking to himself. "Then I'll scare him so bad, he'll shit his pants."

"How, Comrade Commander?"

"I have a very simple plan. When he wakes up, I'll tell him that if he doesn't confess his intentions to escape, I will have him drowned in the river."

Hearing this, I almost fainted for real. I knew he could do it. Who would ever hold him responsible for my death? Nobody. They would simply file the case away.

"We can't do that, Comrade Commander," gasped the sergeant. "We already notified the secret military police about his identity. What if they want to look into the circumstances of his death?"

"Nobody would scrutinize us, Sergeant. This is Communism. Nobody will investigate the death of a traitor. He drowned in the river. Period. It is not our responsibility that he wasn't a very good swimmer. Now, do you understand my trick?"

Of course he understood, poor sergeant. I understood it clearly too: a murder would be committed, made to look like an accident.

Hearing all this made me feel quite rotten. I didn't fake unconsciousness any longer. What for? I couldn't remain fainted forever. Best to get it over with and let him execute his murderous plan, because he was not going to break me. I pretended I was just waking up. I looked around with a confused, dumb expression, as if I hadn't heard any part of the previous conversation.

Noting that I woke up, the commander clapped his hands.

"Well, son, you gave me a real scare. I thought you died without experiencing the last great thrill that I could enrich your life with."

I knew what he was referring to, but I just looked at him with wide-open eyes, as if I had no idea.

"Well, son, I won't beat around the bush for long. Are you willing to write your confession or not? Yes or no?"

I knew this was my last chance. My time was up. *Yes* meant five years, or more! *No* meant suffering for a few minutes, and then death. My hate toward the commander burst into such a fire inside of me that even though I was losing either way, I felt myself the winner. I felt I won, because I decided on *no*.

I started to talk, somewhat shakily, with nervousness.

"Comrade commander, I can't satisfy your order. Or rather, I have already satisfied it. I have confessed everything. I wrote down the truth about this unfortunate mistake. I am innocent. This is all a misunderstanding. I am innocent. After this, Comrade Commander, do what you deem right."

Hearing this, he stared angrily into my eyes. I stood his stare calmly. It was all over. I had nothing to lose anymore. Whatever I had left wasn't worth much in the commander's eyes. It was important for me, though, for it was my human dignity.

"Sergeant, take this idiot down to the yard, and wait for me there."

"Yes, Comrade Commander." The sergeant clicked his boots.

Morosely, he took me down the hallway and out into the yard. We waited there. Both of us knew what was ahead of us. To change the direction of the events, all I had to do was, to say yes. But how could I do that, when the *yes* would be a hundred times worse than the *no*?

In the next few seconds, my whole unhappy life passed in front of my eyes—the life that was so miserly with happiness, yet gave away misery in such abundance.

The rumble of an engine woke me from my gloomy thoughts. A Land Rover turned into the yard from behind the corner of the building. The commander was sitting in it with two guards. They stopped, and the commander ordered us to get in. I looked up at the sky. My thoughts tried to find their way to God.

Merciful God. Is this the end you had planned for me? So I have to die young, by the hands of others? My God, help me! Don't let my life end in such a degrading way. Help me ... help me ... I kept repeating my thoughts. I was hoping for some biblical miracle. No miracle happened, but we were getting close to the river.

How fast we covered the distance, I thought sadly. It had taken me several sweat-soaked hours to cover the same distance from the river to the barracks.

The sergeant looked at the yellowish water of the river with disgust, while the guards looked at him, perplexed. The ignorant soldiers didn't know yet what was ahead of them.

Finally, the vehicle stopped by the riverbank. The commander crawled out. There is no more respectful way of describing his exit from the vehicle, for he was so fat. He surveyed me with a cruel smile. His hate was glowing from his face. Partly because he couldn't break me and partly because I was Hungarian. When he got tired of looking at me, he spat into the river and ordered the soldiers.

"Soldiers, take this traitor into the river, and put his head under the water."

The two soldiers stood there, frozen, motionless, as if they hadn't heard the unbelievable order. The commander, understanding the situation, yelled at them with irritation.

"Didn't you hear me? I said push the traitor's head under the water. This is an order! Move it!"

The two soldiers held my arms timidly and took me knee-deep into the river. I looked into their eyes and saw tears glistening there. Poor, innocent soldiers. They obeyed the barbarous order against their will.

"Move it ... move it!" The commander belched at them.

The soldiers looked at the sergeant, but he was standing with his head hanging low, trying to avoid their eyes. It seemed as if only his body was present. His inner self, along with his mind, seemed to have floated away somewhere so he would not have to witness the upcoming crime. The two soldiers looked at the commander again, hoping to change his orders.

Hoping that it was only a joke. But, unfortunately, it was not a joke. The commander reached for his holster and opened it with deliberation.

"Well, what are you waiting for? Move it or you'll get a bullet yourselves."

There was no way out. The two soldiers, like machines, pushed my head under, and the world ceased to exist for me. What did I feel? These were the most horrible moments of my life. I tried to hold air in my lungs as long as I could. It could not have been a very long time, though, before I felt my mind turning off, and everything turned black. I sensed a strong roar in my ears, as if I were standing under a waterfall. The roar was getting louder and louder. It felt like my inside was ready to explode. My lungs were screaming for air, so I opened my mouth. Instead of air, water gushed into it, and I started to swallow. I thought the end was there, when the soldiers suddenly pulled my head out of the water. I was gasping for air with fitful coughs and grunts, but only for a second, because the commander ordered my head under again, and my agony started all over. I don't know how many times my head went under, for I lost half my consciousness.

Finally, the commander must have gotten bored with the entertainment, because the soldiers dragged me out of the water and threw me on the bank. They waited for a while, till I came to, and then they put me back into the vehicle and drove back to the barrack. There, they took me again into the devilish little red room. Now I started to suspect the reason for the color. Everything was red so it wouldn't show if blood squirted onto the walls or ceiling during interrogations. Who could say your blood was on the wall? How could you prove the red was your blood? Did you want laboratory tests? It was only paint. At least, most of it. This is Communism. The wall is red, case closed. They could kill you there; all your blood could be oozing on those walls, and you could still not say that was your blood making the walls red. That would be an allegation of wrong-doing. Against Communist officers! Well, future will tell what is true and what is allegation.

Important, however, was the present, and the commander in it. He would not let a single minute fly by in peace. He wanted to torture me in every moment. If not physically, then with words. I couldn't quite pull myself together, when he started up again.

"See what happens if you are stubborn? You are simply going to die."
He answered his own questions.

"Now listen to me, you … I don't even know what to call you. I am
going to leave you now until evening. Maybe the water cleansed out your
brain. But listen carefully: I'll come back in the evening again, and if you
are still saying no to me, you are going to say no to your life, for I am going
to forget your head under the water permanently."

He had finished his message to me, and he turned to the sergeant.

"Sergeant!"

"Yes, Comrade Commander."

"This jerk should get no water and no food of any kind. You understand?
Let him fast; he deserves it."

The commander finished his order and left the room, waddling on
his fat legs, his pig-like head swaying back and forth. By God, he seemed
like the very devil to me. I looked after him and wished him to go to hell,
where he belonged, amongst the demons.

I stayed in the room with the sergeant. I figured I could measure the
rest of my life in hours. He had made up his mind to break me.

The sergeant was looking at me ruefully, pondering my fate. My choice
between black and white—only those two, no other shades from the
richness of the rainbow.

"Listen, my friend." He started to speak softly. "In a half hour, my shift
is up. I won't see you again until the evening, when I'll come back with
the commander. I wish I could get you out of this, but the law is the law,
even if it is rotten and unfair. Think over what you plan to do. You have
enough time till then. I sympathize with you. I feel truly bad for you. I
can only advise you to write that confession and admit your intention of
escaping. There is no other way out for you. You are at a dead end." He
stopped, waiting for me to answer.

"I can't do that! Whatever happens, I'll insist on my innocence."

"But this is idiotic. For one, the commander knows full well that
you didn't get lost in the border region. You wanted to escape Romania.
Second, his egotism knows no bounds. He does not know the word *lose*. He
only knows *win*. And third, if you insist, he will keep his promise. There
were other cases before. They were simply filed as accidents. Believe me,
there is no other way out."

35

"I can't do it." I interrupted the sergeant's flow of words. He was wringing his hands nervously.

"Listen, my friend, it is still better in prison than being dead, isn't it?"

"Yes, in general, it is better in prison than being dead," I agreed, "but this does not apply to Romanian political prisons. There, in five years, they turn you into a crippled, insane refuge of a human being."

"I have heard that too," he sighed. "So it is right, what they are whispering about?"

"Yes, it is. My friend is the witness. He was caught trying to escape. He was not strong enough. He had written his confession and got five years. After five years, he is out now, but in what shape! He will never again have his full faculties. His body is crippled, and his mind is abashed."

The sergeant didn't know what to say after this. His head hung low, and he fiddled with his watch. He must have felt I was right. Finally, he looked up, with a bitter little smile in the corner of his mouth.

"My friend, you are very brave. I don't think I could be this strong in your place."

"That is why I don't try to force you to do any more."

"Decide according to your conscience, and let's trust in the help of God."

With some nervousness in his voice, he sounded as if he was accusing himself for being part of these shameful events, even though involuntarily. He checked his watch again and then hit his forehead.

"We have hardly any time left, and I have almost forgotten the most important thing. Be very careful with the guard who takes the shift after me. Whatever he tries to get out of you, with whatever tricks of kindness, resist, for he is a double-dealing traitor. It would be best to pretend you are asleep. He won't wake you up. I'll try to help in that."

He wanted to say something else, but suddenly, we heard footsteps from the hallway. We looked into each other's eyes, sad and frightened. Gently, we shook hands.

"God be with you, my friend, and don't forget, you are sleeping."

I took his advice, and I quickly went to the far corner of the room. I sat down on the floor, rested my head on my pulled-up knees, and pretended to sleep.

In less than a second, the door opened, and the replacement guard entered.

"What's new?"

"Nothing much," my sergeant friend answered.

"Is he sleeping?"

"Yea, unless his mind has already left him permanently."

"He deserves it, whatever he has gotten. All of his kind should be exterminated. Traitors."

"You are right." My friend the sergeant consented, slammed the door nervously behind him, and left the room. The double-dealing new sergeant will never know the real reason behind that bang.

I stayed in that crouched, uncomfortable position for an hour or maybe more. Every part of my body was numb, and I felt a thousand ants crawling in my soles. I was very hungry, but I suffered more from thirst. I knew I could not pretend to sleep much longer. I tried to stretch it out as long as I could, but I felt worse by the minutes.

Come what might, I thought, and I abandoned my sergeant friend's advice. I lifted my head and moved my numb arms and legs. The double-dealing sergeant looked at me with a dumb expression, as if he had seen a miracle.

"So you woke up, you maggot?" he asked rudely.

I didn't give him an answer. He obviously didn't demand one from me either. He was too busy reading a letter to have any interest in starting a verbal sparring with me. He sank back into the letter immediately, breaking into silly giggles every once in a while. As he finished it, I shuddered. Now he was going to start harassing me. But I was to be disappointed, for he started to read the letter over again. He kept reading and giggling. It must have been a love letter. I sighed a sigh of relief. *Good, just keep on reading. At least you leave me in peace for a while,* I thought.

You can never be completely happy, though. My biggest problem was my thirst. My throat was dried out and burning like an oven. My lips were cracked.

Where could I get water? I had been in the bathroom before, so I knew that there was no sink there. It was unsanitary, but who cared. The important thing was that the creatures like me, who were tortured here, did not get water.

A spark of a new sentiment, so far unknown to me, started to make me feel disgusted with myself. How disgraced I was, how humiliated I felt. It is hard to put into words what I felt.

The humiliation I had suffered started to make me feel as if I were shrinking physically. The walls of the room, the floor, and the ceiling seemed to close on me. Along with the room, I was getting smaller and smaller too. Eventually, the room was the size of a matchbox and I was no bigger than a pea inside. How do you face your fellow human beings again after this? When you have been reduced to the size of a pea, you are afraid that someone who has had enough of the whole charade will step on that pea and finish it forever.

It was more than that; this was my own doing. By letting my imagination shrink my surroundings, and myself within them, I had created the scenario of my destruction.

Never, never allow your imagination to shrink you to the size of a pea in the eyes of others, for if you do, they will step on you without hesitation. When you feel the shrinking in your mind, fight your imagination to face the destroying force. Kick the walls of the room and demolish the shrinking structure that is the creation of your sickening mind. Reduce it to rubble, and go out of it to face humanity with dignity like a human, not a pea. Don't ever shrink! Remain human among humans.

I felt I was shrinking, losing my value, becoming nothing.

No! I can't let my last stronghold disintegrate. I need strength to keep fighting. I can't beg for food or water, for that would be the start of giving up, of me beginning to shrink. I have to get water, but not at the price of my dignity. But how? From where? Oh, God! I thought.

Then the idea came to me. The tank of the toilet held water. *It may sound disgusting,* I thought, *but I will drink from that.* It was better than nothing. It was a good idea. I only had to wait for the sergeant to finish reading the letter one more time.

Soon enough, he finished, and before he could start it again, I called to him.

"Comrade Sergeant, I am sorry to bother you, but I have to go to the toilet."

He looked at me, startled and dumb.

"The hell into your innards," he said. "You didn't eat, and you didn't drink; what the devil do you want to shit? Do you want to get rid of your intestines?" He laughed at his cruel joke.

"Well, move, you idiot. What are you waiting for? Applause or a parade? Go!"

He escorted me to the hallway. He followed from behind and kept poking me.

"Keep moving, slow poke."

Just keep talking, idiot, I thought. *Poke into my ribs; do what you want.* The important thing was that I accomplish my plan. As we reached the door to the toilet, he grabbed the shirt on my chest, opened the door with his free hand, and shoved me inside. Then he hollered after me.

"Hurry up, empty the air out of your innards fast, for I don't want to wait for you till the evening."

I closed the door of the toilet. I lifted the cover from the tank, carefully, so I wouldn't make any noise. And there in front of me was the marvelous water. Greedily, I took some into my cupped hands and drank as joyously as if it were the clearest mountain spring. I felt the strong taste of chlorine, but what did I care? All that mattered was that it was water. I washed my face. The water felt good on my swollen cheeks. There was no paper, so I pulled my shirt out of my pants and dried my face with it. I heard the sergeant hollering outside.

"Hurry up, you rascal, or I'll come in after you."

I quickly swallowed a few more mouthfuls and then put the cover back on the tank fast. This sergeant was crazy enough to come in after me. I opened the door calmly and walked out into the hallway. The sergeant stared at me and my wet shirt with vacant eyes. It must have been too much for him to make the connection.

Crudely laughing, he pointed at my shirt and asked, "Hey, you. What happened to you? Did you work up a sweat? I bet it is hard to shit air out of an empty belly." His loud belly-laugh echoed through the long corridor. I stood there feeling grateful to God for sending this moron my way.

My hope flared up again. An unexplainable confidence and unreasonable strength surrounded my heart. It made me understand that when everything seems to fall apart, when you do not see any way out, God is there with you and won't let you lose. From that moment, I forgot about my imaginary shrinking, about the pea I was fast becoming. I was reborn—a human, in the protecting hands of God.

I felt a great weight being lifted from my back when finally, the door opened and my friend, the sergeant from the morning, entered the room. The new shift had started.

In a way, I was glad to get rid of the loud, taunting sergeant whose mockery started to become unbearable. On the other hand, I felt a great sadness overtaking me. Not fear, just sadness, as I realized that my hours were numbered by reality, not imagination.

I felt a great void in my head; then an unfamiliar voice started to fill the empty space. This voice was repeating the same sentence over and over again. *"You are going to die. You are going to die. You are going to die."* As if a grandfather clock was ticking. I was getting faint and dizzy, so I thought I was really about to die. My dizziness was getting stronger. Finally, I realized this was all from hunger. I was close to fainting when I heard the footsteps approaching from the hall.

These steps made me forget my hunger. I had played my role to the finale.

The steps were getting closer and closer. I pulled all my strength together so I wouldn't show any weakness.

The door opened and the familiar company entered: the commander and the two soldiers who had involuntarily practiced how to drown someone on me.

The commander surveyed me with his murderous eyes. He must have been satisfied with what he saw, because he rubbed his hands together and acted as if he had a great surprise for me. He did not leave me in suspense for long. He pulled out a sheet of paper from his pocket and handed it to me with sarcastic formality.

"Read it, son. Take your time, and read it carefully, two or three times, or as many times as necessary. Decide on your reply only after that. But don't forget, this is your last chance."

I started to read the paper and almost collapsed from horror. There it was, black on white. I was dead. It was the report of my suicide. Everything legal and official, signed, witnessed, stamped, and dated. This lie of lies stated: "We tried to save the victim from the river; however, due to the fast current, the rescue operation was unsuccessful. By the time the rescue squad brought him to the bank, he was dead."

I held the paper incredulously. My face must have mirrored my shock and fear, for the commander said in a gratified voice, "Well, son, are you satisfied? As you can see, I didn't waste my time. My thoughts were with you all day as I prepared this little surprise for you. And now, you know what to do," he continued as he pushed a sheet of paper in front of me.

I looked at the paper without a word. I then lived through one of the hardest moments of my life. Everything depended on a simple little *yes*. I tried to envision the life this *yes* would grant me.

Seeing my hesitation, the commander tried to help me with the phony fatherly concern in his voice.

"Look, son, you really don't have to think that hard on this one. You do not have much of a choice but to say yes. Write down everything related to your attempted escape. In return, I will tear up the report about your suicide, and we will forget it. It never existed. If you don't do this, you are truly crazy, since you know damn well what is ahead of you. You can be sure it will happen as I had promised, for I am a man of my words. So, you might as well start, son, and get it over with."

I had no hope. I was wavering, ready to give up, when I heard footsteps from the hallway again. The steps were coming closer, and something inside of me was insisting that these steps were bringing about my deliverance. How could a sensation so contradictory to reality exist? I don't know, but somehow, it does exist—some superhuman strength that gives hope to your brain only at the end, when you are standing at the edge of the cliff, when only seconds separate you from the plunge. That is when this extraordinary strength comes, orders your last seconds to stop passing, and flickers a spark of hope into a living flame in your mind.

I heard the approaching footsteps and experiencing a surge of hope, and I changed completely. I stood up from the table and said to the commander boldly, "Comrade commander, apply your lawful authority over me. Do with me whatever you want, if that is the only way to satisfy your lust for cruelty. I insist on my innocence."

My speech was followed by a second of stunned silence in the room. Only a second, though, for then the commander jumped up from the table and slammed his hand on it so hard that the sheets of paper were flying all over.

"You rotten dog, do you think I am going to waste my time on you? Just you wait, you bastard. You will wish you could take back your words, if you still have time for that. But you won't. Your time is up."

He gave his order. "Take him to the river right away."

The soldiers on duty took me from either side, and my friend, the sergeant, shaking his head in disbelief, opened the door.

Then the surprise came. Two men in civilian clothes stepped into the room, blocking our exit.

"Comrade commander, we are from the secret military police," one of them announced. "Our order is to take over the prisoner charged with the attempted border crossing." He handed some official-looking paper to the commander. He read the paper with the red face of a turkey. The plain-clothed men were studying me in the meantime. They seemed surprised. One of them couldn't resist turning to the commander, who was still reading, and he said to him, "Comrade commander, I believe you have no authority to torment the persons apprehended while attempting to cross the border illegally. That is our job. I see you have given a good workout to this scoundrel."

"We had no choice. This dog resisted," the commander lied. "Do you want them to beat up on us? We treat all prisoners well here." He continued his fabrications. "We feed them, house them, and then wait for your department to come and pick them up. But this jerk," he pointed at me, "as I said, he resisted; he was disrespectful, even threatening. He struck one of our soldiers who was on duty, protecting the laws of our country."

To validate his lies, he asked them, "Do you want me to call in the witnesses?"

The plain-clothes man waved with his hand carelessly.

"There is no need for that. We believe the Comrade Commander."

The commander nodded his head in relief and looked at me with piercing eyes. I looked into his eyes and smirked insolently at him.

He must have understood my expression, for I could see the cold, impotent hate in his eyes. He would have torn me to shreds, given half a chance. To calm himself, he turned to the plain-clothed detectives.

"Say, comrades, how come you are taking him early? Pick-up time was indicated only for tomorrow morning."

"That is true, but the department head ordered him to be picked up tonight. We don't know the reason either," one of them answered with a shrug of a shoulder.

Nothing else remained to be done but the signing of the transfer papers. This gave me a little time to say good-bye to my friend, the sergeant, through some unobserved eye contact. He was the only person there who had been good to me. I looked at him, smiled, and said thank you with my eyes for his kindness. He understood, for his eyes smiled back. He seemed to say, *"It was nothing, my friend, only human decency."*

Then one of the plain-clothes men said, "Let's go!"

At that moment, this short order sounded sweeter to me than all the treasures of the world. Before I left the devilish red room, the stage of all that cruelty, I sent another friendly glance toward my friend, the sergeant, and another "go to hell" look toward the pig-faced commander.

In the yard, the two plain-clothed detectives put me into a Land Rover. The engine roared and the vehicle started to move slowly, leaving behind one of the most barbarian places I have ever been in my whole life.

The vehicle was swallowing kilometers faster and faster. We were getting further and further away from one hell but also getting closer and closer to the secret military police. *Oh, God, stay with me,* I thought, and despite all my efforts, I fell asleep.

The car's brakes screeched loudly, and I woke up, frightened from my dreams. We had stopped in front of a dark, unfriendly building. The heavy, iron-barred gate was locked. It opened only after security papers were checked. This vehicle rolled in, and the heavy gate closed again behind it. I knew the dark building looming in front of me was nothing else but the dreaded secret military police headquarters. I wondered what was in store for me there. It was not likely to be anything pleasant.

The two plain-clothed men didn't waste much time with me, but they didn't hurt me either. That probably was not their duty. They led me into the dark building, then down a long corridor. Left and right, hardwood doors followed each other at an even distance. They were all closed, hiding the objectives and the secrets of the rooms. We stopped in front of one of the doors. The door opened, and we entered a dim room. They did not spend much time with me. One of them said curtly, "You'll stay in this room till tomorrow morning. Take a rest; you could use it." They started toward the door. At the door, he stopped and let his partner ahead. He raised his threatening hand toward me and said in a cold, meaningful voice, "Just a warning: don't you try to sneak out. Don't even move in this room, or you'll be worse off than in the hands of the commander. I hope you understand me."

I wanted to stammer something, but he didn't wait for my answer. Closing the door behind him, he left. But he did not lock the room. I knew I had to be a complete idiot to even think about escaping from there. It would be truly impossible. He must have left the door unlocked as a trap. I entertained no ideas about escape. Instead, I looked around.

To my great surprise, I found a bed! I could not believe my eyes. There was also a toilet and a sink! They must have mistaken me for somebody else. I was fearful for awhile that they would come back and take me into some hole in the cellar. But nobody came. I did not need much encouragement. I washed up to my waist. The cold water was burning my raw cuts and bruises, but ah, how good it was to feel fresh water on my body.

And the bed! It was only a simple little cot, but as I lay down, I felt I was sinking into a silk-covered featherbed. An indescribable pleasure enveloped my tired body.

I felt fairies floating down from the heavens and surrounding my bed. I sensed them stroking my face and my hair and sighing light, healing kisses over my wounds.

Then the fairies brought flowers onto my bed. They kept bringing more and more flowers, until I was all covered with them. The room was filled with the fragrance of the spring flowers, and the fairies were singing in soft, sweet voices. My eyes filled up with tears. One fairy bent down to me and wiped my tears away with her hands.

"Don't … don't," she pleaded in a sweet, soft voice. "Your mother has sent us to you to comfort you in your dire condition. You have suffered a lot. Time has come for you to be happy. We are taking you with us, to where there is no more cruelty, no more blackmail, no more torture, only happiness and leisure."

I was actually afraid, for I saw the fairies picking up my bed, and flying with it toward the clouds. As we reached the clouds, though, my fear dissipated. I felt happy and free. I experienced happiness like never before in my life. I was casting flowers all over the earth from above. I wanted these flowers to be seeds of peace and freedom for mankind all over the world.

The fairies were cheering and laughing happily; they flew higher and higher with my bed, all the way to the stars.

All of a sudden, everything became dark, and the fairies flew away, frightened and screaming, leaving me among the stars.

I didn't know what happened. I looked around, alarmed, and almost yelled out in fear. The commander was standing at the foot of my bed, with two great horns on his head and flames shooting out of his eyes. I huddled in the bed, shaking, and tried to cover myself with the blanket. Then I realized that the blanket had turned into skeletons. I broke down and began to cry, and the commander burst out in a laugh so wild that all the stars fell down.

"See, you scoundrel? I caught up with you, didn't I?" he said while flames poured from his mouth. "Now there are only the two of us. Nobody is going to get you out of my fist now. I'll drown you, bastard."

He reached out his hands to grab my neck. I jumped off the bed and leaped out of the sky with a loud scream. I was still screaming as I woke up. I looked around, terrified. *What happened to me?* I only started to relax a little as I realized it was only a dream. The damn pig-headed commander was haunting me even in my dreams.

My clothes and the bed were soaked. This dream really made me sweat. I got up to wash myself. I knew I would not be able to go back to sleep again after this dream that had started so nicely ended up in such horror.

I had no idea of the time, for the room had no windows. I had a hunch, though, that it was already morning. I was right. As soon as I had finished washing, which was again a painful experience because of my many open wounds, a soldier came in. He was wearing the uniform of the secret military police. He didn't yell at me and was not rude. He simply said, in a calm voice, that he was now taking me to an officer in the interrogation department.

What will happen to me today, God only knows, I thought. The soldier escorted me through the corridors, turning left and right, up and down from one floor to the other, opening doors with buttons and secret codes, confusing me to the point that I would not be able to find my way out, even if I were let go.

There was no elevator in the building. Or if there was, it was not for my benefit. My legs were ready to give up; I was so worn out from hunger. I had a sharp pain in my stomach and my head was throbbing, as if my heart had moved up there. I could not believe how feeble I had become in just a few days. I felt that if this meandering lasted much longer, I was going to faint. Fortunately, the soldier finally stopped in front of a door and knocked.

After a yes from inside, he opened the door and let me in ahead of him. I looked around uneasily, expecting that I would see tools or torture prepared for my interrogation. There was nothing nerve-racking in sight, and that calmed me down somewhat. The room seemed like a standard office rather than a room for forced interrogation. A middle-aged officer was sitting at the desk. He didn't want to notice me. He was studying the objects spread out on the desk in front of him. They were things taken from me at my apprehension.

I started to study him. He had strong facial features, and he could not have been older than thirty-nine or forty. His broad shoulders and athletic body indicated great physical strength. Even though he was sitting, I guessed that he was a good head taller than I was. He wouldn't need any torturing tools; he could swallow me in one piece.

I started to search my brain for some polite opening words, so I would not wake up the sleeping lion in him. I was still indecisive on the greeting, when he looked up with surprise. He stared at me for a while and then, as if he suddenly remembered something, he said, "Please, sit down."

I sat down on the chair he offered to me. He got up, went to the soldier standing guard at the door, and said something to him. I could not understand, for he was speaking very softly. When he finished, the guard left the room.

The two of us remained. He came back to the desk, sat down, and continued to scrutinize me. I didn't know what to expect, but I started to feel that I was more afraid of this officer than I was of the miserable commander.

There was something in his cold stare that said, *"Don't lie; I can see into you."* I was afraid of that.

Finally, he broke the silence and said in a polite, calm voice, "I see they have done a number on you, taking over some of my responsibilities too."

He waited for a while to see if I would answer, but when I didn't, he continued.

"I know they scared the daylight out of you, and now you are afraid of everything. You don't have to worry about me, though. I won't beat you up, if for no other reason than that there is not more room on your body for further abuse."

I looked at his face and tried to find out how honestly he had spoken. His face seemed to show true empathy, but my fear was still holding out. This kind of expression could be a trap.

He lit an expensive Chinese cigarette and offered me one also. I turned it down—partly because I was very hungry and partly because I didn't want to risk it being hit out of my mouth again. This, I had told him too.

"Comrade colonel, not too long ago, a cigarette was offered to me, and then it was hit out of my mouth, so that my head almost went flying after it."

He snickered softly and then turned to me seriously.

"Son, I won't do anything like that to you. If I wanted to hit you, I wouldn't offer a cigarette; I'd just simply beat you to death. It would be a shame to waste a good cigarette. But let's leave this. Tell me, instead: Why did you want to escape from Romania through the Hungarian border?"

Here it comes, I thought. *Now he wants to trick me.* I was trying to be alert and simply said, "I didn't try to escape, Comrade Colonel."

"Of course you wanted to escape," he said, with some nervousness in his voice. "You wanted to escape as truly as I am a colonel. Don't try to deny it; I can see into you."

Well, if he could see into me, he was right, so I waited his blows, without the cigarette. But his hands remained quiet, and he continued.

"I am not going to try to force you to admit it, for I know what I know. You seem like a smart fellow, but you are using your brain the wrong way. Didn't you think that even if you had succeeded in crossing the Romanian border, you would have had to face unknown difficulties at the Hungarian border? Furthermore, if you managed to cross the Hungarian border too, you would have had to walk across Hungary and try to cross the Austrian border. Did you have plans for all these, too, son?"

His speech was a well-planned trap. I had to watch how I was going to answer.

"I didn't plan for any of these, Comrade Colonel, because I had no intention to escape from the country."

"All right, son, have it your way."

I was uneasy about his giving up so easily. It almost seemed as if I was asking the questions from him. Something was cooking, and I was sure it would boil over as soon as the fire gets a little hotter.

"You see, son," he continued, turning up the fire some, "with your escape attempt, you have violated the laws of our country. The laws may be right or wrong, but we have to abide by them, and you have to admit that you have done something wrong. You have tried to follow an impossible road. You might as well resign yourself to the fact that your dream will never come true. If you had a sparkle of hope about your chances, you would suffer far more than what you think this dear freedom is worth to you."

He stopped to rest and looked at me with imploring eyes. He was talking too kindly, almost as a friend would, and I really didn't know what to say. I wetted my lips, swallowed hard, and said, "Comrade colonel, I don't want to offend you with my opposing reply, but even if I did try to escape, I can't admit that to you, for you are colonel of the secret military police. I can't do anything else but to deny the allegations against me."

The colonel slapped his hands in surprise.

"You have guts, and you talk well, but don't get carried away. I have methods to get the truth out of you. Methods that are so effective that you would admit acts you didn't even commit. However, you are already a wreck, and I don't have the heart to hurt you anymore. Do you understand me, son?"

Of course I understood him perfectly. Even though I wasn't the timid kind who was ready to roll over at the first sight of trouble, I clearly felt my significance in front of him. This was not a matter of showing off, not comparing skills in a brawl. This was a question of authority, and all the authority was in the colonel's hand. He could do with me whatever he pleased, without my having a chance to even sigh out of opposition. The laws of the country were behind him, while I had nothing as an acceptable excuse or explanation.

An inner warmth spread through my body from his kindness toward me. He was authority himself. He could crush me like an insect under his boots. He didn't do it. I felt an inner cry. The tears didn't come to my eyes; I could hold them back, but inwardly, I was crying about his humane treatment of me. I was about to express my gratitude when someone knocked on the door.

After the yes from the colonel, the door opened, and a young woman stepped in, wearing a military uniform. She brought some food, put it down on the desk, and left.

"My lunch," the colonel said, as if he had owed an explanation to me.

I surveyed the food on the tray with barely disguised excitement. *If he is going eat in front of me, I would be better off with a good beating,* I thought. I stared at the food greedily and swallowed hard.

"How long since you have eaten?" he asked.

"Since I was apprehended."

"You are holding out well," he said and pushed the tray in front of me. "Eat," he ordered in a harsh voice.

I started to eat wolfishly, as if I had never eaten in my life. Every bite increased my respect for him. He must have belonged among those few people in Romania who did not lose their humanity when they got their rank. Or who knows? Maybe he felt the same way I did, only his high military rank prevented him from expressing it. He had pledged loyalty to the Romanian state when he took the oath. He had promised to uphold the laws of the country, to protect Communism even at the price of his life. Had he broken this oath, he would have been sent in front of the firing squad.

———

I was sitting with a full stomach, enjoying the aroma of the fine Chinese cigarette that the colonel offered. He was filling out some papers with a concerned expression on his face. Finally, he finished, put down his pen, and looked at me gravely. I knew he had broken the law for me and that it was difficult for him to explain what had happened.

There was a deadly silence in the room, as if even the walls would have known that what had happened here had to remain a secret forever. Finally, the colonel broke the silence.

"Son, you are smart enough to know that I broke the law on your behalf. Instead of the interrogation, I have treated you well. I don't expect tears of gratitude. It was only a small percentage of human compassion. I was trying to ease my own conscience for my other sins. Tomorrow morning, you will be back in your hometown. They will not accept you with open arms. You never admitted guilt in what you were charged with. It may not even be considered a sin by God, but it is considered a crime by the Romanian court. You could easily get six months of jail for being caught in the border region, even if they never can prove your intent to escape. But that is their problem. I have completed my job. Listen carefully. Nobody, not even your closest friends, should ever find out how I have treated you. This must remain a secret between you, me, and these walls. Do you understand me?"

I nodded to show I understood.

"Then listen again. I filled out the papers that will follow you to the court. They state that throughout the interrogation, you have insisted your innocence. I am forwarding your case as unproved allegations. I could not make you appear innocent, for you have been apprehended in the forbidden region of the Romanian border. If I regard you as innocent, it would appear suspicious and would get us both in trouble."

He stopped, lit a cigarette, and smoked silently for a while with his eyes closed. He appeared to be lost in thought. Suddenly, he looked at his watch and said, as if he had forgotten who was sitting in the room with him, "Yesterday, about this time, my wife had a little, healthy baby son. I hope when my son grows up, he won't follow my road, but I don't wish him to follow your road either."

"Congratulations, Comrade Colonel. May God protect your son and your family. Your kindness toward me raises you to a much higher rank than a colonel."

"Who knows?" He sighed.

Suddenly, he changed his tone, as if he had just realized the situation.

"Never mind, son. We are actually enemies, based on our circumstances. Remember that most important thing. If anybody asks how were you treated in the secret military police, say, 'Sadly enough.' Make sure you never change this phrase. Do you understand?"

"I do, Comrade Colonel."

"Furthermore, nobody should know that you had food here, or had a cigarette. That is as serious a breach of the rules as is the laxity of the interrogation. Do you understand?"

"Yes, Comrade Colonel, I understand."

"This is all. I hope you have committed it to your memory forever. Finally, let me give you good advice. Not as a colonel, but as a fellow man. Don't ever try to escape from Romania again. You would be caught, and next time you won't get into my office, even if I would try to take your case. And believe me, my colleagues doing the same job I was supposed to do won't treat you the way I did. They would not only break your body but also remove your mind from your head. They were trained to do that. For them, it is better that an anti-Communist person is at least half-mad when he leaves. When he is half-mad, he won't spread dangerous ideas about freedom anymore. Take this as a fatherly advice."

"I'll do that, Comrade Colonel, but if I ever find the road to freedom, I'll break my promise."

For this, the colonel didn't answer; he just shook his head incredulously.

"They will come to pick you up soon, and that will be the end of our contact forever."

"Comrade colonel, thank you for everything you have done for me, and—"

At this point, he stopped me. He put his finger onto his lips and whispered, "Don't forget, son, according to our lifestyle, we are enemies." By the time he had finished his sentence, the door opened, and two soldiers entered.

"Take the prisoner to the waiting room," he ordered in a cold voice.

The soldiers got on either side of me. I sent a last, grateful glance toward the colonel, thanking him one more time for his kindness and humanity. He was no Comrade, no heartless Communist toward me. He was a noble gentleman.

My hometown! This was my first thought, when I reached Maroscasarhely again. My reentry, however, didn't bring me joy. It only brought utter calmness after all the suffering. It was sad to see the familiar streets and all the hundreds of people enjoying their freedom—even if this freedom was only the kind allowed by a Communist government. Still, they were more free than I was. When I dreamed, I imagined real freedom, not this kind of handout. Still, I watched them, with an aching heart, from the barred window of a prisoner car. The fairy castle of my dreams was in ruins. It seemed utterly impossible from that wagon that I will ever be able to rebuild that dream castle again. Everything that happened to me was so horrible, so incredible, that I still could not quite accept it.

I was home in my town, but still, I wasn't home. I couldn't go home to embrace my dear parents or my little kids. I could not shake the hands of my friends. All this caused such heart-wrenching pain that it is painful to remember, even now.

Then, the events started to move really fast, almost like a film played on fast-forward. These events, though, are not worth mentioning. They were nothing but boring steps in the Communist bureaucracy, following rules and regulations that they did not always understand themselves or often got mixed-up about. Whenever this happened, they just made a new rule to cover up the mistake. The only standard was that all the rules were made against the innocent population, with the message "Shut up; don't bark" in this case, or "Shut up; don't bark" in that case. That's why people say that eventually, all Communist bureaucrats become petty tyrants with laws of their own.

On the assigned day, I would face these petty tyrants in the courtroom. They were going to examine me for the crime I had committed and dole out my punishment also.

Was I guilty? For them, I was. Without seeing too far into the future, I knew to expect that clemency from them was as easy as squeezing water out of stones. Individually or together as a group, they all had hearts made of stone. They did not look at the innocence of the person in front of them. Their only concern was to secure their own future at any price.

When time is ripe for the people to say that they have had enough of them and they burst out of the twine of the Communists, blood will flow. They will be willing to sacrifice thousands of innocent people rather than risk their comfortable positions of power, where nobody ever held them responsible for anything. They can kill, torture, imprison, and crush people without hesitation if that's what it takes to keep their positions. But for how long? The answer is somewhere in the unknown future.

On the day of sentencing, I knew my fate ahead of time, without much talent in fortune-telling. I was found guilty simply because I was captured in the forbidden border region. Even though I never admitted my intent to escape, I was guilty, because I had no business being there. For this crime, I was sentenced to a six-month jail term, which meant hard labor. Added to that was a year of probation afterwards, during which I was not allowed to leave town, and I had to appear at the police station once a week. If I did not adhere to the conditions of the probation or committed any minor violation of the law, I would automatically get two more years in jail.

This is how my first attempt to reach freedom landed me in prison. My longing for freedom caused all my pain and suffering. With a heavy heart, I also have to admit that all the harassment and humiliation my family and friends suffered was because of me. I, alone, was the reason—with my restless longing for freedom, my boiling blood, and my inability to bow in front of the terrible Communist machinery.

As I recalled the events during my quiet contemplation in the cell, I realized how costly freedom was. Though the events sometimes seemed more like nightmares than reality, they were real. I also knew that my fight was not over. Who knew how many more nightmarish events my future held—events that would not be not illusions but the reality of my life, my destiny leading toward freedom.

During the long days in the prison, I had plenty of time to analyze the mistakes I had made during my escape attempt. This occupation helped me forget where I was, and time seemed to move faster too.

Even though the prison was an assembly of filth, junk, starvation, beastly labor, and exhaustion, as well as a breeding ground for infectious diseases, God was with me and protected me from all these dangers.

When I only had five more days left of my term, I disdained all the misery I had suffered, and I was happily looking forward to the future.

Not that I forgot the cruel treatment I suffered from the Communists, their false allegations, or their crushing the rights of the people. I had made a solemn promise to God and to myself that when I got out of prison, I would never surrender to anybody. I would not become a snitch just to clear myself in the eyes of the Communists. I would never give up my fight for my freedom. My need for that is a vital ingredient of my blood. I can only give it up when the last drop of blood leaves my body.

I knew, and felt it inevitable, that as soon as I was out of prison, I would start planning my next attempt at escaping Romania, trusting in God and myself.

After my release from prison, I stepped out through the prison gate into a cold, overcast day. I had to lean against the wall for a second; I was shaking so violently with excitement. I was free! I was standing under the cloudy sky, a free man. The cold wind grabbed my light summer jacket. I turned up my collar and looked around, hoping someone would come with some warm clothing and help me home. I did not have to wait for long before I spotted my dear father. As he reached me, he helped me into the coat without a word and held me in his arms lovingly.

"Oh, my son, I could not wait for you in the prison office. I was afraid I would attack somebody to revenge your treatment," he said, wiping the tears from his eyes.

"I understand, Father," I said softly, and my eyes filled up too.

We had a lot to talk about; still, we walked alongside each other in silence, each of us buried in his private thoughts. Dear Father! He had always understood my love for freedom. He might even have felt responsible, for he sowed the seeds of it in my soul. He had raised me valuing it above all. He had been through thousands of dangerous situations, too, during the Second World War. His sufferings would fill another book. He was taken to the front as a very young man. He became a prisoner of war in Russia, and he served four years of hard labor there. It was a miracle he came back, for many thousands had perished. He must have longed for freedom from that camp.

I felt a very strong spiritual unity with him as we walked quietly together. The only difference was timing. He had fought his battles for freedom in the past, and I was fighting them in the present. Poor Father! He had lost his fight. He had never reached his freedom. He had come back from the camp, but he was stuck in Communism. He had spent his life slaving for Mother and for us. I dragged myself ruefully next to him and realized just how much I loved him—and how much I pitied him, too, for his wasted life. As we walked, I put my hand into his, as I did when I was a little child. Though outwardly a grown-up, I became a child again as he held my hand and we walked to where love was waiting for me.

The touch of his hands gave me inner strength, but feeling the hard, callused palm also increased the pain in my heart. This hard palm had been following me since my childhood. Many things had changed around me since then, but the palms of my father remained the same. It hurt me, for I knew that his hand did not get hard while counting money. It was the hard work from morning to night that did it. This was my father, toiling, struggling for his family all his life. I could have bellowed in my pain.

I wanted to scream out loud for the world to hear that every word of the Communists is a lie. I wanted to trudge their red flag, which they respected more than God, into the mud and stomp on it with both feet.

This, of course, was just imagination, fueled by my inner fury. It was not likely to happen. Even if in the future, the people trudge the red flag into the mud, where would I be by that time? Would I be long dead? Would I be a free man? Would I rot in another prison somewhere? Who knew?

Whatever my future held, let it be. I'd accept the consequences. I had guts, and sooner or later, I'd make it through. I'd get out of the suffocating hoop of Communism. I failed the first time, but I'd keep trying. I owed this to myself, but also to my loving father.

There was great rejoicing in my parents' home when my mother, my sisters, and my brother saw me. I have a tough constitution, but I was sobbing uncontrollably when my mother embraced me.

"Oh, Mother, dear! How are you feeling? I thought I might never see you again!"

"My little son! Did they hurt you a lot? Don't you worry, though. Now that you are home, I'll take care of you," she said, softly caressing my unkempt hair. Finally, my father succeeded in calming her down. He helped her into a chair before she might faint. She sat down and drank some water, but she didn't take her eyes off me. Her eyes still brimmed with tears, and she kept repeating, "What did they do to my son? The Communist beasts. What did they do? What did they do?"

My sisters were crying also, and they were gazing at me incredulously.

"What happened to them?" I asked my brother as I shook his hand and we embraced. "Why are they staring at me?"

"You are surely a sight to behold, Brother," he said mournfully. "You look like a skeleton. They really did a number on you. If I didn't see you with my own eyes, I would have a hard time believing someone could be reduced to this, just for being against the Communist system," he said pensively.

I put my hand on his shoulder, looked straight into his eyes, and said to him, "Brother, you have to fight and you have to suffer if you want to get out of this dictatorship. You won't get out on a flying carpet, as they do in fairy tales."

"But is freedom worth all the suffering you had gone through? It is quite possible that you will never reach it, or you could pay with your life trying," he said nervously.

"Who knows? Maybe it isn't worth it," I said, "but I can't tell you for sure until after I am a free man."

My brother didn't answer, just shook his head pessimistically. My dear brother! Since I was two years younger, he forever tried to protect me. We loved each other as brothers, but we always fought about his efforts to save me from possible danger. He did not want to flee with me. He would rather suffer in Communism. Maybe he just gave up meekly, as millions of others did. He became a little part in the giant machinery. Connected with the other millions, they were working like slaves to keep the machinery moving.

I was different. I wanted to become what God had intended me to become—a human being! A human being with a soul, someone who can control his destiny according to the decisions of his heart, and most of all, who can think freely.

My poor brother did not understand this. Or maybe his self-respect had weakened so much that he had no more strength to fight the system. How much I pitied him and loved him at the same time.

God bless my mother! As the days passed, I slowly recovered under her faithful care. I was glad to leave the torture days of prison behind me, but a sad, bitter expression still remained on my face. The medicine for that did not exist in Romania.

My parents could see my sadness day after day and knew there was nothing they could do about that. I was an alien, pushed out, someone who had no future. I only had a present that was going to remain with me till the end of my life.

Not too long ago, my body had been aching from the harsh conditions of the prison life. Its deep scars were still on my body and mind, yet as they were slowly fading away, my mind was still wandering again on the roads toward freedom. The road was still obscure, for I could not come up with any reasonable plan for my escape. My mood was like the weather, one day bright and sunny, the next gloomy and rainy. I had to wait quietly for a new plan to emerge.

The long idleness was driving me out of my mind. I could not go out anywhere. I had some touchy reasons for that. First of all, my friends said, "Look, Paul, we can't associate with you anymore, lest we, too, become marked men by the police. We have to live our lives here. We are very sorry, but you have to understand this."

Of course I understood. I never bothered them again with my friendship, though tears swelled up in my eyes when, seeing some old friend, instead of reaching my hand out to him, I turned my head and crossed over to the other side of the street.

Then there were my enemies. They recognized me, and being conscientious Communists, made a point of provoking me every time they saw me. They harassed me, called me names, even spat as they passed me, humiliating me painfully. I could have beaten them up, but I was on probation, so I had to endure everything, lest I end up back in jail. So I bore it and suffered, though at times I was very near to a good fight with these faithful Communists. Fortunately, my mind was always stronger than the fury urging my fists. This saved me from two additional years in jail.

I spent most of my time at Anna's, my girlfriend. She did not quite understand me, but she accepted me as I was. It was strange. She knew it as well as I that we were never going to marry, and this topic never came up either. We were not in love with each other; we were only really good friends. We gave each other everything a man and woman could give, without tying each other down or making promises. Was this sinful? Maybe, but I didn't feel it that way. We did not betray each other by giving to our bodies what man and woman can give.

I was hurrying to her just now also, feeling my blood heating up as I thought of her long, wavy brown hair. I loved to bury my face into this hair for long minutes. It had the fragrance of wildflowers, which made me feel as if we were lying outside, in the woods somewhere, among the flowers. All this meant freedom to me. I could not explain it with words, only with my soul, the utter satisfaction this brought to my being.

It could also be possible that Anna was a substitute for everything that my ex-wife had slowly forgotten to give me. This led to painful alienation, which hurt me mostly because it meant separation from my two little girls.

I felt lonely and deserted. Fate had cut my life in two. I had nothing in my future.

Maybe that is why I stayed with Anna. When time would come to depart, I wouldn't be breaking up a sizzling love affair or abandoning our future. It would hurt, but the coming years would bring healing and forgetting.

―――――――――――

Days and months passed quickly through my year of probation, and I became more and more restless. I felt the time nearing when I would again let my mind loose on the preparation for my next attempt.

The recent months had brought many unexpected events that left a great emptiness inside of me. Why talk of happiness though? It had avoided me from my earliest childhood years. It could have been me, though, avoiding *it*, disgusted by its inequality evident already in school. Kids were treated according to the importance of the position their parents occupied in the Communist system. Free vacations, camps, trips, everything—I was always left out of these childhood pleasures. My teachers made it clear that I was the child of suspicious, anti-Communist parents.

I paid no heed to them, though, because I loved my parents and thought my mother and father to be greater persons than any of the infamous Communist presidents. During my unhappy childhood, I never blamed them for my misfortune. I looked up on them with great respect for their courageous fortitude in a Communist country, where they didn't belong but were forced to stay.

My poor mother was born in the still-free Transylvania, in a family of small nobility. She lived in carefree comfort until Communists came, stripped the family of everything, and threw them out on the street.

My father's story wasn't any more cheerful. His father, my grandfather, was a traveling wholesale merchant until Communism came and pocketed all his possessions for the government's needs. He was not giving up his holidays willingly, and he broke some Communist bones in the process. For this, he was sentenced to five years in jail, where his fierce anti-Communist conviction was thoroughly broken.

The old saying goes, though, that "blood will never turn to water"—not even in Communism. My parents and grandparents suffered great material as well as spiritual losses, but here I was, fighting still in my blood. I wanted to reach freedom, not only for myself, but for the sake of my grandparents, my parents, my brother and sisters, and for everybody in Communist countries who goes to bed at night and wakes up in the morning with the yearning for freedom. I wanted to prove to all these people that yes, you could achieve freedom if you were the president in your struggle. I wanted to prove that no system exists that can successfully hold down the human spirit and force on it circumstances that contradict basic human rights and morals.

I had one more week left of my probation. Suddenly, I felt the film was set on fast-forward. Things started to happen at a surprising speed.

I was at my ex-wife's, visiting my daughters, Claudia and Astrid. They were delighted to see me. Poor little things! They were too young to understand what had happened between their mother and me. They were happy to see me, to feel in their heart that they, too, had a father. They might not see him every day, but when he came, he always had a surprise for them.

This is what I had become. A "holiday father." It was not a decision I had made alone, but in my heart, I had certainly blamed myself and would have given a lot for a chance to be together again. But it was too late for either of us. We had learned to walk alone.

The last sparks of love were gone. What remained was only respect. Even that was mostly on my part. After the recent events, my wife's esteem of me was on its decline. I tried to explain that to fight for your freedom, suffering imprisonment for your striving is sad, but not despicable. If she would only check history books, she could find heroes by the thousand who fought for their personal freedom, or for the freedom of their countries. Their fates should evoke respect rather than scorn. She did not understand, nor did she agree. She considered me a criminal who had broken the laws. This did not bother me too much. In fact, I thought she might say that, to express her anxiety for me, to steer me away from my plans. Who can see into the woman's heart?

I did not try to explain myself, or force respect from her anymore. It was enough if I could see my little girls. I loved them dearly. For their sakes, I had wavered several times, considering giving up even freedom for a chance to stay near them for the rest of my life.

Unfortunately, my fate was not that. All thoughts of the possibilities of my staying home were erased from my mind one day, when a conversation with my ex-wife made everything clear.

My daughters, Claudia and Astrid, were sleeping peacefully, having reached the land of sweet children's dreams. They were dreaming about castles full of flowers, happy princes and princesses who had found each other as they fled from evil and founded the country of happiness. In this place, all good people were honored and allowed to stay and live happily ever after. They would be compensated for all the suffering their bodies and souls were subjected to by evil forces.

I looked at them for a while, and tears slowly filled my eyes. They'll never know that their father was weeping for them. I could not remain there too long, for I felt fury swelling up in me in the place of helpless bitterness. I was ready to howl in my pain. For all misery in my life, I blamed the inhuman, humiliating Communist system.

I closed the door of the bedroom and collapsed into a chair by the table with a swimming head. I was like a felled young tree. My ex-wife put a cup of strong coffee in front of me without saying a word and looked at my prematurely graying hair.

I fiddled with the cup and tried to figure out how best to start what I wanted to tell her once more. Finally, the words came out slowly, with great difficulties, sealing my future also.

"You know, Hannelore, I pondered a great deal about what had happened between us, and I feel we did not have a serious enough reason to get a divorce. What do you think?" I asked her imploringly.

She turned her large, green eyes at me seriously and answered with a slow, rueful smile.

"You may be right, Paul," she said, "but it is too late to change anything."

"Think of the children, though! I am not asking you to fall in love with me again. I only want to be a father to my kids."

"This is nice of you, but you should have thought about that before you acted against the laws of the country."

"Whether I acted against the law or not is not the question now. I am still the father of my children."

"Don't even try this, Paul, for it is not you but what you have done that prevents us from ever getting back together again. I don't want my innocent girls to be harassed by remarks about their anti-Communist, traitor father. I would rather stay separate."

"Is this your last word, Hannelore?"

"Yes, it is. I have to think of the future of the kids. I will have to raise them to become good Communists, so they can rectify the mistake of their father."

"I am embarrassed to hear all this from your mouth! After all, you have been my wife! You are humiliating my whole family! Raise my kids to become good Communists? There isn't a single Communist in my family," I cried out with nervous surprise. I could not have felt more pain from the stab of a knife, than from the words of my ex-wife.

She looked at me coldly and finished the conversation. Her answer was a dead-end street. It allowed no reply.

"I'll do what I said, Paul, for I'll have to rub off the tarnish you have smeared on their name and on mine."

This was more than I could take. I felt my attempts were pitted against a stranger, a woman I did not know, one with a heart of stone.

Deadly tired, I stood up. With my last hopes dissipated, I felt unbearable coldness around me. I knew there was only one warm place here, the room where my kids were sleeping. Their love toward me was this blessed warmth.

My hand was on the front door when my ex-wife touched my arm. Automatically, I turned around and looked at the person I once loved dearly, with feelings of total defeat in my heart.

She seemed determined to finish with me, for she gave me a final blow.

"Listen, Paul, I'd rather if you came to see the kids less frequently. I am not comfortable with your visits, and neither are others. It would probably be best if you moved to another city. That way people would forget about you and what you have done. Don't you think?"

"Sure, you are right. I'll come once more to say good-bye to the children," I said pensively. By the time I could have expected an answer, the door closed behind me. The last thread that might have kept me from another attempt to escape was served.

I hurried through the streets, half-mad. I was going to my parents. They were the only ones who still understood and respected my longing for freedom.

Rain was pouring from the pitch-dark sky, as if mourning for my tortured soul. The cold rain felt good. It cooled off my raging blood and soothed the throbbing pressure in my head. I wasn't far from my parents' place. I had just turned the last corner when two strangers stepped out of the darkness and stood in my way.

I had no idea what they wanted, but I stiffened, for I felt they must have had trouble on their mind. I could not see their faces in the darkness, so even if they were familiar, I could not tell. They might have known me; if not personally, they could've recognized me from the papers. The taller one came and faced me; the shorter approached from the side. The tall one addressed me.

"Well, you stinking anti-Communist. We'll teach you now to appreciate Communism."

"You'll remember this day for the rest of your life, you traitor of a pig. That is, if you'll still live after this lesson." The shorter one completed the promise.

My blood boiled over in a second, for I wasn't a namby-pamby myself in most of my life either. I was about to answer with some degrading remark of my own when the taller one leaped at me. I was not quite prepared for that. I barely had time to bend my upper body out of the way of his hand, in which a shiny object glinted. Still, I could feel the knife, for I saw it right as it lightly cut my chest on the left side. Lucky for me, the cut wasn't deep. I did not feel much pain, only a small trickle of something hot.

It was enough, though, for blood to cloud over my eyes and I showed them that I could throw good punches myself. I was aiming my blows precisely at the throat, the stomach, and other sensitive body parts.

It was not a long skirmish. When they saw they were defeated shamefully, they started to run—if you could call the pitiful limping that. I didn't go after them, though I could have prepared them for emergency medical treatment. However, my human dignity would not let me do that.

Instead, I looked sadly after their shadows as they disappeared in the dark. Pressing my hands on my softly bleeding chest, I wondered how low people could get.

The shadows were gone and, worn and depressed, I walked home to my parents. This was the only place in the world where the warmth of love was waiting for me. They embraced me with worried love and tenderness.

My parents had a real fright seeing my blood-soaked shirt. I seemed to have a serious injury. When I took off the shirt and my father examined the superficial wound, they calmed down some, though mother could not stop weeping.

After my father dressed the wound, I told them honestly that I was planning another escape attempt in the near future. I told them about my visit and the conversation with my ex-wife. I explained that I couldn't live artificially separated from my children. I would rather be far away from them. I also brought up the incident in the street. This could be considered a warning for the future. I was lucky this time, getting out with only a minor injury, but where was the warranty that tomorrow, or the day after, or a month from now, some overzealous Communist wouldn't cut my throat. If I protected myself and fought back, I would rot in jail for the rest of my life or would simply be executed. As my final argument, I added that I not only don't *like* Communism, I detest it with my whole being to the point of being sick. There was not a cure for my illness here. Matter of fact, it was getting worse and worse every day.

My father nodded his head approvingly, and though he looked sad, he didn't say a word. Mother, my dear sweet mother, could not do anything but weep uncontrollably. She could not believe that after all the suffering, I would choose that road again.

Poor Mother! Her cries were more painful to me than my wound. I sat down next to her. I wiped off her tears with my handkerchief, and I kissed her hands—the hands that raised me, rocked my cradle, did the laundering and ironing for me, put food in front of me, and did all the good things for me. These one-time aristocratic hands that used to flutter over the ivories of the piano.

My tears swelled up too. I understood her and admitted in my heart that there was no other woman in the world who had suffered as much as my mother. I caressed her hands and explained to her why I couldn't stay home, though the separation would be as painful to me as it was to her.

She understood everything. I departed with a goodnight kiss, and my heart was tortured by guilt. I knew I had caused her pain again that would be with her for the rest of her life.

We talked for a while longer with my father, and then, as he started to prepare for the night, I asked him to try to console my mother when I wouldn't be around her anymore. He didn't say anything, just nodded with tears in his eyes. His look seemed to say, *"How, Son, how can I do that, when I am not assured myself either?"*

I went to bed, though I couldn't sleep. I started to despair, asking myself, why did I have to be born at all? Only to cause sadness to my parents? Sleep slowly closed my eyes, putting off this unnatural question to be answered by the future.

The old saying goes that once bad luck becomes your companion, it'll stay with you till the end of your trip. I didn't believe those old sayings, but I'd started to wonder lately.

I went to visit my friend Anna. I wanted to pour out my misery to her. I felt grief was sufficient for half the population of the town.

When I got there, I noticed that she was not greeting me with the familiar friendliness. Some cold fright was in her eyes, and she acted as if we were only casual acquaintances who had just recently met.

I knew there was trouble here. I asked her to tell me honestly whatever it was that disturbed her. She did not need much prodding before she started to talk openly.

She admitted that she was afraid because a few days earlier, she had been visited by the secret military police. They were inquiring about me. They wanted to know the nature of our relationship and whether I revealed anything to her about my future plans. They asked if I ever spoke against Communism in front of her. After this harassing interview, they left, giving her the advice to stop seeing me unless she wants to get in trouble too.

I wasn't surprised. This was one of the basic methods of the Communists, trying to control everybody's private life.

It was very hard for Anna to say this, I know. She was a simple woman who had no luxurious dreams or longings for this unknown thing I called freedom. She had to live her life here under the Communist flag, stripped from her basic human rights. She wanted to live her ordinary life in peace, not harassed by the secret military police. She asked me to break up our relationship. It was never more than a friendship anyway.

My poor, dear Anna! Tears rolled down her face. She could hardly believe that after being support and help for each other during the hard times and sharing our occasional happiness, we had to separate to the order of someone else. Of course, we did not have to obey this order, but if we were real friends, why would we want to cause problems for each other?

It would have been mostly Anna who would have a hard time. She could lose her job, could have been interrogated and harassed in countless ways because of me. I was known to be a restless discontent.

I did not want her to be disturbed unjustly. I knew I could repay her unconditional goodness toward me if I honored her plea and left her.

It was painful to think that we had thrown away our friendship as a bone to the hungry Communist dogs, but we had to do it. This was the only way to secure her future.

We spent one last night together and then went on our separate ways, like brooks flowing from the same spring, following different courses—one slow and steady, the other fast and violent.

I never saw Anna again. Sometimes I felt a burning desire to see her again and smell that fragrance of the wildflowers in her long, brown hair, but I knew I had no right shattering her new life. I would only tear open painful old wounds. May God help her to find the right mate. She certainly deserved it.

Having lost everything, I calmly turned all my attention to the preparations of my new plan to find the road I would have to follow to reach my freedom. I knew my plans had to be exact and accurate. There was no room for mistakes. No cracks to fit the tip of a needle through, or I had signed my own death warrant.

Trusting in God, I made my preparations enthusiastically.

Part Two

T he old proverb says that your enemy is frightening until you start to know it, whether it is man, woman, or wild beast. I don't know if everybody agrees with this, but I certainly felt this way. My first attempt to escape from Romania failed, and I had terrible memories of the punishment I received as a result. These were meant to make me timid and fearful for the rest of my life, but they didn't. I became bolder.

I learned to be more careful and take every minute detail into consideration. I also realized that it was harder to do it alone. I felt the need for a partner with whom to discuss my plans and shoulder the hardships, to share the success or the failure.

The time had come to put my plans to motion. My year of probation expired. I wasn't exactly considered spotless after what had happened, but I could move about with more freedom, without the constant surveillance.

This was all I needed. I cranked up the machinery, hoping that this time I would sail over the barriers, however high and dangerous.

I was sitting in a bar with my brother on the outskirts of the town. This was not a place the secret police frequented, and the few regulars, looking for their happiness in a drink or two, paid no attention to us. We were drinking strong cognac and strong espresso.

I had thought about it, and I picked my brother to be my partner in my next attempt to escape. This is what I wanted to tell him. In theory, everything was so nice and smooth. We would escape together so it would not only be me, but also my brother who would gain his freedom. But it was in theory. To come out with it and tell him in reality, I needed my second cognac. I swallowed hard and softened my voice.

"You know, Brother, I decided to try to flee from Romania again." I waited for him to say something, but he only stared at me as if he were seeing a ghost, so I continued. "I thought you and I ought to do this together. What do you say?"

"Not a bad idea, but what about my family?"

"I have a family too," I answered.

"Yes, but you are separated from them. You are divorced, and with all the political trouble you have gotten into, it is just as well that you are no longer with them. Believe me, Paul, I don't want any trouble for my wife and children."

"That is fine, Andy, but think about it! If we succeed, we can give our families a better future."

"*If* we succeed ... Paul, this sounds like '*If* I had money, I would buy a car,' or '*If* I could sing, I would be a star'. This word, *if,* is what separates dreams from reality. You have to understand, Paul, that I can't build my future, the future of my children, on dreams."

"Everything is a dream until we put actions into motion to make it reality," I answered, with some nervousness in my voice.

"Make it reality, just like you have done. Think about it. Think real hard about what you want to do again, for this 'freedom mania' of yours caused difficulties for not just you, but—let me make a list here—your parents, sisters, me, everybody close to you. Is that what you really want, Paul?"

"I don't want to cause trouble to you or to anybody else, Brother, but don't expect or ask of me that I give up my plan to get out of here."

"I don't want you to give up your plans, Paul; I just want you to know the facts. Do you know that after your first attempt, the secret police came for me at two in the morning? They got me out of bed. Didn't give me a chance even to get dressed. They dragged me to the station, where they interrogated me for ten hours. The same thing happened to our parents and sisters, and God only knows how many other people who were close to you," he finished nervously, in an accusing tone.

I was physically hurting inside, hearing this account of the events. I knew he was right. He was telling the truth. I did cause a lot of problems for him and his family. What else could I do, though? Should I give up my plan to escape? An invisible force was pulling me. At that moment, I hated myself. I felt I was wicked for causing all this distress to everybody. But I also knew that this precarious situation wouldn't change until I managed to get out of Romania. I asked my brother Andy, one last time, hoping he might change his firm stand.

"So you are not coming with me?"

"I would like to, Paul, but I can't do it. Please understand me. We are brothers, and I love you very much, but our characters are different. We are two rivers, flowing to different directions from the same source. You are wild, destructive, fearless, and your heart is made of stone. I am slow, mellow, and loving. Am I not right?"

"But of course you are," I answered with forced cheerfulness. "You have analyzed us perfectly. Let's have another drink, then, for God only knows when we will drink together again."

"Don't go, Paul. I am going to miss you so. You are my little brother," he said softly, with tears of true brotherly love glistening in his eyes.

I grabbed his hand and held it real tight, trying to express my love and gratitude. Something was welling up in my eyes too, because the single light bulb of the bar started to take on the colors of the rainbow. We emptied our glasses and left.

As we walked home, we embraced and sang melancholy songs, pouring out the misery of our souls. In front of his house, we stood for a long time, holding each other tight, not knowing if this was our last chance, or if we were ever going to embrace again. This may be a farewell for a year, or for five or ten years. Who knows the secrets of the future?

I left my brother and turned toward home. I felt so lonely, as if I were alone on the whole Earth. I was walking home with my head hanging low and started wondering—maybe the problem was not with Communism. Maybe it was me. Looking around me, I saw millions of humbly quiet people. I was the only rebellious discontent, fighting for justice that may not even exist anywhere. Or does it? I longed for freedom, but maybe it was only a fiction written about in books. Does it really exist anywhere?

Idiotic thoughts. I tried to purge them from my mind. This softening was caused by the conversation with my brother. I couldn't break! I couldn't retreat. I started a fight for freedom and for justice. There was no way back. There never would be. There was only one road.

I cleared my mind from the mushy sentimental thoughts and became once again what my brother had said: adamant, with a heart of stone. I turned my thoughts back to the pressing concerns of the plan. Whom should I pick as a partner for my escape? Who could do it? Names and faces floated in front of me, like on a movie screen. I categorized them, scrutinizing every individual thoroughly. Finally, I had only two of my best friends left on my roster, Michael and Lazlo. They were the "real thing." They were going to be my partners in my next attempt to escape from Romania.

———————————

In the little room, the smoke was thick enough to be sliced with a knife. The table was littered with brandy glasses, coffee cups, maps, rulers, scrap papers, and ashtrays full of cigarette butts. My friends Lazlo and Michael were sitting, deeply engulfed in their thoughts, staring at the mess on the table. My plan of the escape had generated an argument, and I was pacing up and down the room nervously.

"I don't know what your problem is with it," I said, starting my explanation again. "I spent a year working out the details of this plan in my mind. I am not giving up easily. Believe me, the best way to get out of Romania is on a freight train."

"I agree with that," answered Michael, "but tell me, how do you propose to open the door of a locked freight car without damaging the seal?"

"Right—that is impossible to do." Lazlo took his side also.

"No, it isn't," I opposed irritably. "Listen up; I'll explain. There are different types of freight cars. We are going to pick one that has little round holes on the roof, beside the regular doors. They use those to transport granular material. Well, I found out that those little round holes are covered with a flap that can be opened, so we won't have to damage the safety seal on the door. It is possible."

Both of them were still opposing me.

"Wait, I'm not done yet," I continued. "These cars are made of a special iron alloy. This is important to know, for later on. Right now, we only have to examine the roofs of these freight cars. They usually have six or eight of these round holes. The holes are positioned in pairs: two, two, two, and two. Now, the flaps can open singly, or in pairs. And this is where the secret is. To open them singly, what you find impossible, is indeed that. I agree. For if we try to open a flap, the safety cord will break, and the border guards will notice and make the assumption that someone is inside, trying to get out of the country. Right?" I asked.

"Unfortunately, it is," they both consented morosely.

"Then grab onto something, my friends, because here comes the big gun." I went on with my explanation. "The paired flaps are connected with an iron bar that has a safety tongue at the end. The seal is connected to the flap, and the iron bar, with a cord of some sort. This is what makes it impossible to open the flap unnoticed, for if you try to move it, this cord will break, and the safety seal will fall off. But! I devised a key, with which I can turn the iron bar, till the tongue at the end will slip out of the clasp. This way, with the tongue out, both flaps could be opened, together with the iron bar, without breaking the cord and the seal. The reason for this is quite simple. If we turn the rod, it won't detach from the flaps; therefore, it won't pull on the cord."

"Are you sure of this?" asked Lazlo with excitement.

"Are you really sure?" repeated Michael doubtfully.

"Absolutely!" I said. "I bet my life on it. There is one problem, though … a … that one of us would have to make a sacrifice for the other two."

"What do you mean?" They looked at me with surprised anguish.

"I'll explain. What I mean by sacrifice is this: after opening the flap and getting into the car, we can close the flap from the inside."

"So?" Michael interrupted me and looked at Lazlo, puzzled.

"Wait," I silenced him. "I said I can close it, but someone still has to turn the rod back into its original position, with the tongue in the clasp. And this can only be done from the outside. Without this, even if the flaps are closed, anybody can see that they have been tampered with."

I took a deep breath and continued.

"The other not very pleasant aspect is that after the third person locks the flaps, the outside world will cease to exist for the two inside. The flaps cannot be opened from the inside, and they could spend days locked in there before the train reaches its destination in France, West Germany, Greece, Turkey, or any other free country, where they admit political refugees. So we'll be locked up, even in those countries, until we make enough noise inside so that someone will open the doors."

"This could be dangerous," Michael interrupted anxiously. "The freight cars may be delayed on different yards for days, until a train is assembled and ready to leave the country."

"You have something right there," I agreed, "but I have looked into that, and I found out that this wait cannot be longer than ten days. I can wait ten days for my freedom."

"You are right. This is the most certain way; I vote for you," Lazlo said finally.

I looked at Michael, waiting for his answer. We stared at each other in the eyes for a while. I thought he still might vote against my plan, but that was not what happened.

"You always could talk convincingly," he said. "I vouch for your plan also, and I accept the job to lock the flaps behind you. It is more important for Lazlo and you to get out of this country. You both have been caught before for your attempts to escape. You have the right of way. If your efforts are successful, I'll organize a party of three the same way and, following your plan to a *T*, we will go after you."

Lazlo and I shook hands with him, touched by his generosity. We felt that few, even among the best of friends, would accept the role he took on. He was more than a friend. He was our brother in this conspiracy, and that meant we would risk our lives for each other.

We took a little break, smoked our cigarettes, and slurped the strong espresso, satisfied with the progress we had made.

We still had to agree on the date and on the station where we were to pick our train. This was no big deal, though, since I had already worked it out in my head. I only had to present it to them and get their approval.

After relaxing with lighthearted chat about women, love, and everyday events, I asked them to follow my announcements closely again, for I was returning to our serious business.

"My friends," I started solemnly. "I think it is time we decide on the date, month and day, of our departure. We should also choose the city that has the most suitable train yard for our purpose. Tell me what you think."

Lazlo and Michael sank in deep contemplation. I let them think quietly. I had a ready plan, but I did not want to hurt their feelings by not giving them a chance to give their opinion. Lazlo spoke first.

"I suggest," he started, "that we leave in June. For the point of departure, Arad would be best. It is close to the Romanian-Hungarian border, and several freight trains leave the country daily there."

"Before I answer, let's hear Michael too."

"I think we should wait until November," he said. "That would give us more time to get ready. I also think the Goloc train yard would be better. It is a port city, and there are more trains going to foreign destinations from there."

"Both plans have good points, but neither is perfect." I took over again. "First of all, Lazlo, the problem with yours is that June is very hot. The iron freight car would become unbearable without windows; there are only little ventilation holes. We could not last more than two days without fresh air. Even if they are transporting packaged goods and the ventilation holes are open, it would not be enough in June. On fine days, the cars standing on the yards are beaten by the sun from dawn to dusk. They heat up so much that we would not survive inside, since we could not open anything once we are locked in."

"I didn't think of that," said Lazlo respectfully. "You are right."

"That is because I have been burned before, so I'm trying to be extra careful. But I have other objections also. The Arad train yard won't work either. It is too large a yard, with too many guards, even military personnel. We would be caught at our first move."

"All right, all right. Don't even continue. You are right."

"As for you suggestion, Michael, the problems with it are more or less the same, only the other way around when it comes to the date. The Goloc train yard is also way too big for our purpose. There are far too many guards there as well. As for the date, November is just as dangerous because of the cold than June was because of the heat. The iron hull of the wagon reserves the cold so much that inside we would feel as if we were in a refrigerator. Catching a cold and having a coughing fit could give us away to the border guards—not to mention how the iron sheets of the hull would strengthen the sound of a cough."

Michael clapped his hands in surprise and said, with honest approval in his voice, "You should be a detective. You have really thought of everything that could go wrong and solved the problems ahead of time. I have to admit, my idea wasn't the best."

"I have to say the same thing again. I have been burned before; so help me God, I am going to be careful this time."

I lit another cigarette and drank some coffee. Lazlo and Michael waited restlessly to hear the rest of my plan. I could see Lazlo was about to say something in his anxiety, so I started to talk.

"Listen, friends, I can see that you are concerned, waiting for my suggestions. Before I tell them, though, I would like you to understand that during our adventure, you have to stop worrying. I am not saying this to criticize you. I was anxious to hear your recommendations. That is natural. But we have to make a pledge amongst ourselves to control our nervousness. We can't let it get even close to us while we are working on our escape. Worry can easily be the downfall of the venture. Worry can cause haste, and carelessness, forgetfulness, and it would gnaw on our bravery and eventually make us timid. We can't allow any of these to overcome us if we want our plan to succeed. There is only one medicine against all these maladies: never to worry."

The two of them looked at each other, somewhat puzzled, and then Michael couldn't resist asking, "Tell me, boss, where did you pick up the slogans?"

I wasn't sure whether he was serious or stuck the word *boss* on his question sarcastically. I wanted to avoid arguments, so I answered calmly.

"Michael, my friend, I didn't pick them up; I have learned them from experience. You know that great generals have lost battles because of nervousness. Traffic accidents happen by the score because of nervousness. The simplest example to prove it, though, comes from the world of animals, which are often thought of as dumb. You know how they are flushed out of their safe hiding places by the noise created behind them. They jump up and run out into the way of the guns, and ... puff! Had they stayed hidden quietly until the hunt was over, they could have saved themselves."

Lazlo must have felt the Michael's remark was somewhat inappropriate and made me a little tense, so he made an effort to soften the situation.

"You rightly called him *boss*; he really should be the one. In this venture, every little detail is important, whether it has to do with our physical or spiritual well-being, for we are playing with our lives."

Lazlo finished his little speech, and Michael said humbly, "Forget about my silly remark, *boss*. I am not as clever and experienced as you are, and if I were a hare, I would have ended up facing the barrel of a gun without your advice."

This picture of him as a hare made all three of us laugh, and that finally released the pressure.

We laughed for a while with abandon, and then I picked up the serious business again.

"Friends, this is my plan of action. The best month to start off would be April. The weather is not too hot or too cold."

"You mean we should wait a year?" interrupted Michael, shocked.

"No," I said flatly, "we are in April now. Today is the sixteenth. We are leaving in ten days, on the twenty-sixth. As for the town, I think Tovis is our best bet. The town is small, so we can prepare for all anticipated difficulties."

"But no freight trains leave from there to abroad," said Michael.

"Yes, they do," I continued. "The town is small, but the train yard is almost too big. Freight cars are sorted there according to their foreign destinations. This is all I have to say, but I want you to think it over thoroughly before you agree. If anything goes wrong, I don't want you to blame me. We have to come to an agreement in all our decisions and share the success or blame fairly too."

There was a long silence after my little speech. I lit a cigarette and thought that if they answered no to my proposal, that would mean that they were not the right partners, and I would have to start looking for someone else. This thought depressed me, but Lazlo spoke up.

"Boss, I thought about your plan, and the more I think, the better it looks. It seems thorough and well prepared. So my vote is yes."

I shook his hand gratefully and looked at Michael for his answer. He was ready too.

"I agree too. I think your plan is a good one. Of course, my role in it is limited. My job will be over after I lock that flap. The rest is up to you. All I can do is to pray for the success of your escape from Romania," he finished, somewhat moved.

I shook his hand too and patted him on the back, tried to cheer him up.

"Don't worry; if we succeed, then, following my plan, you can come after us too. Just never forget to keep your nerves steady. Believe me, I know firsthand how important it is."

They both knew the sad experiences I was referring to and why I didn't care to repeat them.

However, what had happened became the past, and in front of me was happiness. I had a winning case. A new plan. I was full of hope.

All that was left to do was to become familiar with the tools. I showed them the key I had devised. I also explained that we would need ten tins of meat and ten liter containers of water. If we projected our venture to take ten days at the most, half a liter of water per person per day should be sufficient. We also needed to take along some formaldehyde, to get rid of our odor. At every border station, the cars were checked with the help of German shepherds to sniff out possible dissidents hiding in them. I also thought we would need at least a hundred small plastic bags. I could see Lazlo and Michael were puzzled about that.

"If our trip will take about ten days, we can not go to the bathroom inside the car. The heat would eventually strengthen the smell so bad that not only would we suffer from it, but the guards outside would smell it too, not to mention the German shepherds. Using the plastic bags in double or triple layers, then closing them tight, would control the smell, while standing in a station somewhere. Once in motion, we can peek out the ventilation holes to check the area and throw the bags out as we travel through deserted parts of the track."

They both admitted that it had never occurred to them that we should prepare for this important factor too.

We discussed some other minor details and agreed not to take any extra clothing. We would wear workman's coveralls over our own clothing, since walking among the freight cars in civilian clothing would be utterly dangerous.

I had left the hardest topic for last: smoking. I insisted that while in the wagon, we wouldn't have a single cigarette. We agreed to smoke to our heart's content until then.

They both agreed to all my regulations. We shook hands happily to seal our friendship and the secret plan. I said good-bye and left.

It was late evening as I stepped out onto the street and headed home. I was happy beyond measure. Mellowed, I looked up to the sky, where thousand upon thousand stars were shining at me. They seemed like diamond studs, celebrating my happiness with their light. They twinkled encouragingly, promising me success in my endeavor. Looking at the stars with adoration, I addressed God.

"Oh, God, you know everything about my plans. You have all the power to decide whether or not I deserve freedom. Bowing my head before you, I accept your judgment."

The twenty-fifth of April! How I wished this day would never come. On this day, I said good-bye to my loving parents, my sisters and my brother, and to my little girls. No words can express the agony I was causing to my parents with this new plan of mine, which I was going to set in motion on the following day. During the last few hours I had spent with them, twenty-four years of goodness and love flowed through my heart—all the goodness and love I had received from them. They tried to create a life from nothing to fill the void of destitution, satisfy the hopeless longing of childhood for goods unattainable (seen only in movies). They soothed away the bruises of my soul caused by the long years of inhumane treatment by the Communists.

Would the pain of the separation from them ever subside in my heart? Was freedom a cure for this pain? I am hard-headed, with a heart of stone, just as my brother had said.

But I longed for freedom, as a child dreams about castles of fairy tales. Something beautiful, something out of reach. Only, I had to reach this castle of my dreams. I had to reach freedom.

We had a farewell dinner at my parents'. I waited for my sisters and brother to arrive. This waiting was sheer agony. The ticking seconds seemed like hours.

There was nothing to talk about with my parents. They knew my mind was made up, and nothing would change my decision. They also knew this meant that tomorrow, I'd start again on a road of thousands of unknown dangers. I tried to console my mother, but how can you soothe the pain of the heart of a mother about to lose her son?

My poor mother! She kept breaking into tears, and she could only say the same thing over and over.

"Paul, my son, you are throwing yourself into great danger again tomorrow!"

What could I answer to that? She was right. Should I have said, *"Don't worry, Mother, there won't be any danger. I'll take my passport tomorrow and have a visa stamped into it to go to West Germany or to some other free country."*

This is the way it should have been, but what a nightmare it was to get a visa to travel outside Romania. There was only one way. If you wanted to get into a free country, you had to try to escape. If you were successful, you had outsmarted the combined cunning of the Communist machinery. If you failed and were caught, they'd teach you a lesson never to challenge their shrewdness.

No, there was no way to cheer up my mother—not even by describing my successful future, however graphically I'd tried.

My father filled up our brandy glasses with strong plum brandy and said softly, "Good luck, Son. May God help you be successful in your venture."

"May God help us," I answered and swallowed the strong drink in one gulp. Dear Hungarian life! This is how we lived. We warmed our hearts and soothed our pain with brandy. You didn't need to drink a lot. Just enough to forget the sorrow and bring a melancholy song on your lips—those heart-wrenching songs that can only be sung by Hungarians.

My father knew quite a few of those songs, and his rich, deep voice had often brought tears into my eyes. He did not sing now, however. He didn't see it fit, and I didn't have the heart to ask him, though I was longing to hear that beloved deep voice once more. Instead, he was studying the key, which I had devised and he had made for us.

"So you want to open the covering flaps of the freight car with this, Son?"

"Yes, Father, see, like this," I tried to show him how I would turn the rod, connecting the flaps. "You did a wonderful job on this key. It is the work of a real master."

"Little help my master hand is, Son. What matters is the design. I just hope you were right."

"It will work, Father; I know it will. I'll be able to open the flaps with this."

"God help you, Son, for you know that if you fail again, it would break our hearts. I might be able to take it, but your mother won't endure the consequences if you are captured again."

"I know all that, Father; I'll do everything right this time. I will be more careful, more cautious."

"I trust you, Son. To some extent, I feel responsible for your actions. I raised you to be strong and independent. I taught you to fight for your freedom. Don't you think, though, that there is a limit to even that?"

"No, Father, or rather, yes, there is a limit, but you can stretch mine until I reach my freedom. Let's not talk about it now, though, for mother is watching, and we are only upsetting her."

"Well, Son, you are right," he said with a sigh. I was relieved, for I had just avoided another argument. It had happened before, several times, that we had serious arguments with my father about the consequences of my actions. He tried to gauge whether the freedom I was so longing for was worth all the suffering. His scale seemed to always tip toward no. I frequently felt, though, that he weighed that side down enormously with his great parental love and concern. I knew how much he had valued freedom; I had learned it from him. I also knew that he loved me more than he loved freedom. He did not want to lose me. He did not want me to be tortured, should I get caught. He did not want my human dignity to be trampled on, and he did not want me to be treated like a slave. All these worries were weighing heavily on his scale, and made him conclude, "It isn't worth it." All this grew out of his great love.

My father was about to say something, but the door opened, and my brother and sisters entered. Suddenly, everything changed. Until then, the seconds had seemed to crawl like hours, but now time seemed to fly with the speed of light. The dinner, which my dear mother prepared in my honor, my last conversation with my sisters and brother, and finally, the heart-wrenching last embrace of my mother—it was all over in an instant. My father's powerful hug; my sisters' kisses; my brother's protective grip of my shoulder; mellowing, tearful eyes—they were all flying away from me with the speed of light.

At least, that is how it felt to me, for I just now felt the full measure of the pain of separation in my heart. We all knew that this farewell was not for just a short trip, bearing with it the conviction of meeting again soon. This was a saying of good-bye between life and death. We may see each other again, but chances were just as good that we wouldn't. That was what was painful. I was not nearly as afraid of the torture and humiliation I might suffer in the hands of the Communists as I was that this might be the last time I would ever see my loved ones. Just one more hug! Just one last kiss! One last "God bless you," and I tore myself away from the place where I was unconditionally loved.

My parents, my sisters, my brother, and I were like a chain, connected by love. And it was I, again, who broke this chain, and as an unattached link would roll alone toward the unknown.

I was standing on the street alone, having one last look at my parents' house. How small it was, but what warm love was living inside it. I knew that in whatever part of the world I would end up, whatever spacious halls of magnificent castles I would visit, the ballrooms with glittering chandeliers—the warmth of the heartfelt love I had left behind in this little house, I would never find again.

I looked at my watch. The minutes did not crawl like hours and didn't fly with the speed of light either. They were ticking away with their ordinary pace. It was midnight.

I turned my back toward the little house and started to walk, as the old ones used to say, toward the unknown future. I was walking slowly as if a strong magnet was pulling me back. I did not turn back for a last look, for I knew, if I did—though my heart was made of stone, according to my brother—it would melt (stones can melt sometimes too), and I would run back into the embracing arms of my mother and ask her to hold me tight, just as she has done when I was a little kid.

April 26th of 1980. Remember this day forever, I said to Lazlo and Michael moved, as we arrived into the town of Tovis. We had come here on the train. This was the most convenient. We could leave our few luggages in lockers of the station, and we started out to survey the freight yard. Lazlo and Michael were following me, since I had been here before, and knew my way around. We were in a good mood, telling jokes, to chase away the boredom of the long walk. The disturbing yard was at least six kilometers away.

Leaving the last houses of the town behind us, we turned on a narrow path. The embankment of the railroad was running along one side of the path, blocking the town from our sight. On the other side, as far as we could see, lay well-tended fields—the handiwork of industrious people. Too bad it was not for their own good, but for the government. We walked on, and we met a little brook cutting across the fields. The sun was beating down with unusual force, and we took long gulps of the water we had carried along.

Finally, we reached the large, earthen dam. It was built to hold back the extensive swamp behind it, which after heavy rains would threaten the railroad bed. Here, I stopped Lazlo and Michael.

"Well, guys, it is time we put on our overalls. We are getting close to the distributing yard."

I put my field glasses in the pocket of my overalls, for I planned to stay away from the yard during daylight and follow the activities only from a distance. I checked on Lazlo and Michael and, seeing that they were ready too, gave out the order to start up. As we climbed over the dam, we could see the vast expanse of the swamp.

"See all this," I asked them, pointing toward it with a sweep of my arm. "This, here, is the territory of the unknown dangers. If someone gets lost in this swamp and gets out alive, it was with the special grace of God."

Lazlo and Michael looked at the swamp with disgust. I didn't know it myself either, that soon enough, we would get a taste of it. We were walking on the top of the dam now. The concert of millions of frogs was accompanying us, which soon became tiresome. There were open water surfaces not covered with reeds, where in the slimy water we could see leeches and water snakes enjoying the shallow water warmed up by the sun. It was rather disgusting. Lazlo and Michael were walking on the other side, looking at the railroad bed and carrying on a discussion about the time the first rails were laid in the country. I let them immerse in the topic, but compelled by some inner force, I was studying the swamp.

As I walked alongside, I noted its direction and other features. I also noticed that the dam was almost twice as high toward the swamp as on the other side, where the tracks lay. At this time, I had no idea, how useful all this information would become later.

I was roused from my thoughts by the distant noise of the distribution station. I looked up, warning Lazlo and Michael also. From the distance, we could make out the railroad yard. We picked up our pace. Approaching the yard, the screech of wagons being transferred from rail to rail, became louder and louder. The diesel engines let out shrill whistles, and soon we could hear the instructions blaring from the loudspeakers.

We were about fifty meters away from the station. The dam, which restrained the swamp, turned away here. As far as we could see, grazing fields extended, dotted with occasional wild fruit trees. We ran down on the slope of the dam, and in the knee-high grass of the field, we tried to get as close to the yard as we could. A big, old pear tree stood about twenty meters from the yard. We stopped there. We lay down in the tall grass, which covered us entirely. I took out my field glass and started to watch the activity in the control tower. I checked out the floodlights and realized somberly that there were plenty of them. They could easily turn the darkness of the night into bright daylight. Countless wagons were waiting to be combined into trains. I was scrutinizing them through my field glasses, when I noticed a chain of about thirty cars on a dead-end track. More cars were being added to them as I watched. I knew that by midnight, the train would be completely assembled, and in the morning, at the latest, it would leave the station. *This is what we need*, I thought. I took the glasses off my eyes and turned to Lazlo and Michael.

"Do you see that row of wagons on the right, where they are adding on the others?"

"Yes," they answered.

"Listen to my plan. We wait until dark. Then we come back here with our luggage. Michael, you will wait here while Lazlo and I go into the yard and check out the tickets on the side of the wagons to find one destined to a free country. If luck is with us and we find one, we'll come back to you. Do you follow?"

"Of course!" they said, so I continued.

"Very well; so, if we find a suitable car, we'll wait until the railroad workers check out the whole train, and then we get into the break-cabin of one of the cars with our stuff. If we can get this far without being noticed, we will have it made. After that, all we had to do is hide in an open wagon, where we can wait out even ten hours too, until the train moves out. We will come out of hiding only after the train has left the town safely behind.

"Then comes the tricky part. All three of us, with the luggage, will have to move from wagon to wagon until we reach our car. After that, we all know what to do. I can't emphasize enough, though, how important it is to be careful as we move from car to car. One wrong move can have fatal consequences, so we must follow each other closely and be ready to help. This is all, my friends." I concluded my explanation.

"All seems clear to me," Lazlo agreed.

Michael was scratching his head.

"What is the problem?" I asked him.

"I understand everything, except, how are we going to recognize our car as we're crawling on top of wagons of a moving train in the middle of the night?"

I could see Lazlo following the logic of the question, and both of them looked at me as if they had caught me unprepared. However, I was always prepared for checkmate, so I smiled with confidence.

"My friends, that is really simple. I didn't say it, for I thought you figured it too. We will count the cars and will know ours by its position from the engine. Let's say we pick car number seventeen; then all we have to do is count the wagons from the engine and find the seventeenth one."

They did not answer but seemed somewhat embarrassed. Finally, Michael cleared his throat.

"I admit we could not get far without you."

"You are right about that," Lazlo consented.

"Of course you would." I shook off their homage. "You might be even doing it better, but forget that now. Remember, we pledged cooperation and help to each other for the common goal. Let's go back to the town now, find a little restaurant where we can eat something and spend a few hours until dark."

Lazlo and Michael jumped up, delighted, and slapped my back with true friendship. I was happy feeling this closeness, for I knew that real friends those days were rare as white crows.

Our hearts brimmed with good hope for the future, and we turned our steps toward the town.

Oh, God! If we only knew the secrets our future holds. We could avoid many black clouds in our lives!

———————————

Tovis was enveloped in darkness. We had been waiting for this darkness. Not as criminals, thieves, or highwayman. No! We only tried to escape under the wail of darkness, from our bitter past toward an unknown future.

From the town, we went back to the passenger rail station first, to get our luggage. We filled the ten-liter container with drinking water and said a final good-bye to the town of Tovis. We started to walk in the darkness of the night. Stumbling over unseen obstacles, we took turns carrying the bags.

After a long walk, we reached the earthen dam and continued on top of it. The great, stinking swamp along the dam seemed even more dangerous and repulsive hiding its unknown danger in the darkness.

The distribution station was still quite a distance ahead of us, but the glow of its floodlights and signal lights were already visible. From a distance, the dark horizon was occasionally split by lightning and low rumbling, like the sound of distant cannons rolled toward us. There was a thunderstorm somewhere in the distance. I didn't like that. The wind blowing into our faces told me that the storm was coming our way. The wind got stronger and stronger and heavily beat the reeds of the swamp, which created the eerie sound of thousand of opponents trampling after us in the reeds.

I knew we could not leave Michael waiting for us under the lone tree. If the storm got there, it would be a prime target for lightning. I touched his shoulder gently and whispered to him.

"Listen, Michael, you can't wait under the tree, as we had discussed in the morning, because of the coming storm. Lay in the grass, at least twenty meters away from the tree."

"Whatever you say, boss," he said amicably. "It is just the same for me whether I wait under the tree or in the grass."

"It may be just the same to you, but not to me. I would not want on my conscience that something happened to you because of my carelessness."

It made him feel good, that I was worried about him. He put his hand on my shoulder, expressing his gratitude more sincerely than he could have done it with words. We were close to the station, and after a few steps, the shape of the big pear tree separated from the backdrop of darkness.

I ordered a stop, and we lay down in the grass. It felt good to our aching feet. After a short rest, it was time for Lazlo and I to start our action. I gave my last instructions to Michael.

"Wait for us in this exact spot. It is ten thirty now. Lazlo and I will search for a suitable wagon for two hours at the most. Whether we find one or not, we will come back after that time. If we are not back, wait for another hour, and if we are not here, run for your life, for that means we got into some trouble. Do you understand?"

"I understand," he answered.

We did not wait any longer. After saying a last farewell to Michael, we took off into the darkness. Lazlo and I approached the station slowly and reached the first cars without any difficulties. Cautiously, we stopped to look around. Luck was with us. We could not see any guards stationed around the first two rows of cars. There, trains were ready to move out, waiting only for the diesel engines. There was no need to hurry, though. The station struggled with a shortage of engines, so I knew the trains might have to wait as much as five more hours for an incoming train whose engine could be used. We had plenty of time to do a thorough job. I touched my friend's arm softly as a warning.

"Let's go, Lazlo. You check the cars of the train on the right, and I'll check on the left. Do it slowly, and be careful. We've got all the time we need. When you are finished, we'll meet here." Lazlo nodded approvingly.

"Let's go then."

We started out, each on his own assignment. The noise from the other tracks was quite loud. Screeching breaks, clanking wagons, the piercing whistles of the engines, as well as human shouts filled the air. It did not worry me, though. Calmly and carefully, I studied the tickets displayed on the side of the wagons, checking out their destinations. I had read a good many of them already. Names of distant cities and towns appeared, but unfortunately, none fitting for us. *Just go on,* I tried to encourage myself, praying to God all the while. Long minutes passed as I moved from wagon to wagon searching, but luck did not join me.

I had no way of knowing what Lazlo had found. I hoped he had come upon a suitable car. I had reached the last car. No good! With a deep sigh, I turned back. My only hope was that Lazlo was luckier than I. As I neared the spot, I could see him already there, leaning against a wagon. His posture showed it, before he could say a word. He didn't find anything either.

"Damn this world," he whispered. "All the wagons I checked are going to Communist countries."

"I found the same."

"What are we going to do now?" He asked, downhearted.

"We have to go back to Michael with the bad news,and come back again tomorrow. There will be a different train here by then. Sooner or later, we will find one. Let's go."

I started to walk back. That is when a big mistake occurred. Lazlo, instead of following me, suddenly climbed through the train to the one standing on the third rack.

"Come back here!" I was going to order him sternly and started to climb through myself, when all of a sudden, a guard appeared from nowhere and faced him. I felt that we were lost. The guard called to us in Romanian.

"What are you doing here?"

"We are electricians," I answered calmly, trying to hide my nervousness.

"Where?" Came the next question.

"Here in the vicinity, sir, but right now, we are between jobs, so we came to look around a little."

"Show me your ID."

If we had one, I thought. Turning to Lazlo, I said in Hungarian, so that the guard would not understand me, "Be prepared to run; that is our only chance."

The guard did not understand what I had said, but that only made us look more suspicious. He started to call for help.

"Mike, George, Johnny, come over here! There are two thieves here, or God knows what they are doing here."

This, we only heard from a distance, for we started to run as fast as we could. Luckily, the station was so noisy that his comrades didn't hear him, so we had a head start. Michael must have sensed, too, that something was amiss, for when we reached him, he simply handed over our bags and fell in step with us. Soon, we heard the yelling of our pursuers, mixed with the barking of dogs. Lazlo and Michael were running toward the railroad bed in panic.

"Not that way," I screamed at them, "follow me!"

I knew that we would be caught easily if we tried to follow the rails. I turned toward the dam. I scaled its side, looking back for a second to make sure they were coming.

"Hurry up, hurry up!" I yelled. They were still a few meters from the dam, and I could already see our chasers, running with strong flashlights and followed by dogs.

When Lazlo and Michael caught up with me, I did not have time to explain anything, so I just said, "Whatever I do, just follow me, and stay as close as you can. Let's go."

I lowered myself into the swamp. I sank in up to my knees at the first step. Lifting my feet for each step was a major effort, but I didn't care. My only thought was to get into the swamp as fast as we could, as far as we could. When I thought we were in far enough, I ordered a stop. I felt the bottom getting softer and softer. I knew it would be dangerous to get in any further. I opened the plastic container and emptied out the water, to lighten our load. After a short rest, we started to battle the swamp again. I was following the signal lights placed alongside the track. I could just barely see the tops of the posts above the dam. This was enough, though, for I knew that this way, we were advancing parallel to the tracks and wouldn't get too deep into the swamp.

The excited barking of the dogs became audible again, and we could hear the humans yelling also.

"Hey, guys, come back! You won't be hurt; just tell us what were you doing at the station. Come back! The swamp is sure death. It's a lot deeper further in; you'll never get out."

I didn't believe them. I knew, if we went back, they'd apprehend us and could find out easily that we were not there to steal anything, but to escape from the country. All they had to do is call up the local police in my hometown, where my first escape attempt was well known. I'd rather choose the swamp than the prison again.

Lazlo and Michael were standing timidly next to me, and I felt that they would rather give up and go back. I had to spruce up their spirit somehow. I tried to encourage them.

"Listen up. I know it seems now that it would a lot easier to turn back now and give up. But you know where that would lead us. Interrogation and prison! You don't want that. So take my advice, follow me, and fight the swamp. If you want, you can go back, but I won't. We have a fighting chance here, my friends. They won't attempt to hunt us down here, because they are afraid of the swamp."

Lazlo and Michael looked at each other insecurely, but finally their courage won, for they turned to me and said unanimously, "We'll stick to you in good or bad, as we had agreed."

"Then let's go!"

We started up again in the thick blackness, trying to make our way by pushing the dense weeds out of our faces. We could hear the barking dogs, and yelling people for a while, but as the distance grew, it became fainter and fainter.

However, our next troubles were just beginning. It started to rain. In a short time, it turned into a downpour. We got soaked in no time at all. The sweat from our wading and fighting in the swamp froze on us, and in the chill of the night, we were shivering uncontrollably. However, I could not worry about my discomfort, or that of my friends either. My only thought was to get far, far away from the damn place of my second failure. I was praying to God, for I could only survive with his help. My plan went down the drain, but I wasn't thinking about that now. The immediate task was to live through this place. The cold rain was coming down hard, without any sign of letting up soon. At some points, my legs sank in up to my knees. The bottom seemed to be getting softer and softer. I pictured the terrible death waiting for us as we sunk lower and lower into the disgusting muck. Sweat of this fright covered my forehead, and I pulled my feet up from the sticky mud with renewed vigor.

Long minutes passed, and we were still alive. Hope started to flicker in my heart again, though our lives weren't worth much at this godforsaken place. I didn't allow any time for rest, though Lazlo and Michael were pleading for it. My legs were close to giving up too, and I felt it from the ever-stronger tremble in my muscles, but by the morning light, I wanted to be as far away as possible from the town of Tovis.

I could see the fifth signal light along the tracks, and since I had counted them as we walked by this morning, I knew that we could not be far from the edge of the swamp. I felt the bottom get slightly firmer, and the muck did not reach quite up to my knees. Thank God, we were getting out of this menacing place. I didn't tell anything to Lazlo and Michael yet, for I wasn't sure myself. Soon the reed was getting less dense, and in the distance we could see the looming dark shape of the earthen dam. I stopped them happily and whispered with excitement.

"Friends, we have conquered the greater danger; we have won over the swamp!"

Lazlo and Michael hugged me gratefully, without a word. Then Michael started to talk.

"Let's clean up a little and get on the train. The sooner we get away from here, the better."

"Let's go!" agreed Lazlo too.

"Are you out of your mind?" I asked nervously. "Don't you think that our enemies are already at the railroad station waiting for us? Don't you think they have the logic to figure out that if we are strangers around here, we are going to hurry to the train station? How can you be so stupid?"

"But what else can we do?" asked Michael in shock.

"This is what we will do," I told them. "We will walk carefully, avoiding Tovis, to the next village. It is not a great distance, maybe five kilometers. We should get there before daylight, and there we can get on a train unnoticed."

"You are right, boss," agreed Lazlo again.

"Of course he is right; only, my legs are hurting so," grumbled Michael concededly.

"It is better if they hurt here then to have them resting in prison," I said, reminding Michael of our precious situation. To avoid any chance of further discussion, I started to walk briskly.

We reached the village. The complete silence was broken only by the occasional barks of dogs. We were soaking wet, filthy, and muddy, but still alive and free. The rain was letting up some as if even it was sympathetic toward our miseries.

Before reaching the railroad station of the village, we stopped at the little brook that cut across the village. We cleaned up as best as we could, taking off the overalls first. Our clothing underneath was not thoroughly drenched. We took off our shoes to clean the mud from the inside, and then wiped it off from the outside too. We were almost presentable. Nobody would have guessed that we were the escapees from the swamp.

As we reached the station, we approached it carefully, but we did not see anybody suspicious. The waiting room was almost empty. A few passengers were snoozing on the benches, and others were chatting softly. I bought the tickets to Segesvar. We had an hour before the train was due, so we could finally rest and have something to eat from the cans we were carrying with us. We were out of immediate danger, but we had little reason to feel happy. My second plan had failed too, after all the planning and hoping.

The minutes passed, and I sat with my head hanging low, sinking further and further into despair. I didn't make it out. Oh, God! I am still here; the Communists still have power over me. I would have to go back, embarrassed, humiliated, an exploited slave among the millions and millions of others, who drag through their lives like mortally wounded animals.

Why? What was I striving for? For equal rights, which were all lies? For freedom, which did not exist? For human dignity, which did not exist anywhere, not even on paper? Why?

I was desperately searching for some answers when I was stirred from my thoughts by the sharp static of the loudspeaker, followed by the announcement that the train would arrive in five minutes. The passengers started to move out to the platform. We went out too, without talking, trying to cover up our nervousness by lighting one cigarette after the other.

The sharp whistle of the train stabbed the cold morning air, and the lights of the approaching engine shined through the distance.

There were few passengers, so we found an empty compartment. We settled in comfortably as the train started to pull out. Gaining speed, it took us further and further from the place of my shameful failure. I was the loser in this round, but I had gained valuable experience. I had learned that I could not control another person's mental state and stability. I was thinking of my friend Lazlo, who was sleeping next to me, all worn out.

I studied his exhausted features and felt pity for him, rather than disappointment. I knew that I had no right to condemn him for the mistake he had made. He had done it accidentally, because of his anxiety, and he had paid for it just as much as Michael and I.

The train sped away with us onboard, and I found as I looked back at it that even the swamp was not as loathsome. Matter of fact, I was sort of grateful, for it had engulfed us and covered our tracks, which protected us from our pursuers. With its putrid muck, it had stopped them from following us. It had opened its gates for us and saved us from prison. I also knew that if God's grace were not with us, we could not have made it out from there either.

My God, how little our human power is in front of you, yet still so many of us turn away from you, I thought. I felt a mellowing inside. Even the rhythm of the wheels on the track seemed to announce God's glory, toward the blessed sun rising in the flaming eastern sky. My heart filled up with gratitude. I was happy.

I was happy, for I could see the rising sun. I was alive; I had escaped mortal dangers; I was free to try other plans, with chances of success hidden in the future.

The train was slowing down. I looked out the window, filling up my lungs with the sharp, fresh morning air. The outlines of Segesvar started to show in the distance. I remembered its bloody past from history.

I woke up Lazlo and Michael who were sleeping sweetly like innocent children. I filed away all the sad memories of the most recent events into the library of the past and greeted them cheerfully.

"Good morning, my friends. Thank God, we are home again."

Part Three

It seemed as if the end of the world was nearing for us. Our closeness was marred by more and more disagreements. Everything was in disarray, and I was afraid that I would never get the full confidence of my friends again. I was sadly missing the calm force of that confidence.

Our situation was rather grim, and the future seemed hopeless. We were also running out of time. We only had two more days left of the unpaid vacation we had taken. We were also running low on funds. We could barely afford cigarettes. Of course, we had the choice of going home to our parents, but I didn't want to do that. I remembered how difficult the last farewell was, after we had told them our intention to escape. It would break their hearts if we made them go through that again. Also, they would probably try to talk us out of our plans, and I was afraid that we would be inclined to abandon it ourselves, too, after this recent defeat.

So, I insisted that we stay in Michael's apartment, claiming that a lot could happen in two days. My friends agreed with little enthusiasm, indicating that it was just the same for them either way. They tried to catch up on their sleep, resting their tired bodies and souls after the ordeal. I could not stay put, though. My mind just couldn't rest while I was in this country.

Leaving them sleeping in the apartment, I went out to town. At the railroad station, I bought the daily *Red Flag* and went into the restaurant at the station to get an espresso. The hot coffee felt good, and as I turned the pages of my paper, I had to smile. The headlines were such incredibly phony lies:

"The Protective Arms of Communism Embrace the Working People"

"Harmony of Equality and Brotherhood, Thanks to Socialism"

"Our Prominence in the World; the President of Romania Works Consistently for World Peace"

"Long Live Our Beloved President and His Wife, Who Has Achieved Unprecedented Well-Being for All in Our Dear Communist Country"

This went on and on throughout the whole paper. I was ready to throw away the paper, when my eyes caught a headline: "Segesvar Textile Factory Achieves Glorious International Success." I started to read the article eagerly. It said, among other things, that 40 percent of the factory's products were exported to Western countries, and it predicted the rosy future it would create for the town as well as for the whole country. The rest of the article was devoted to praising the Communist leaders as protectors and benefactors of the general public. I wasn't much interested.

What an idiot I was! My chances were right under my nose, and I was, meandering in other towns, facing unknown problems. I left the station eagerly and walked to the loading yard of the freight trains. The wagons must have been pulled up only recently, for trucks and vans were still parked next to each other for the unloading of merchandise. I was delighted; I knew that this meant at least some would be soon loaded up again.

I didn't go home just yet to tell the good news to Lazlo and Michael. I didn't want to risk anything by being hasty. I wanted to make sure that everything would work this time. For a few hours, I loitered around and watched the comings and goings of the international trains. Their happy, carefree passengers waved to me through the windows. After a few hours, I returned to the freight yard. I saw quite a few wagons that had been unloaded in the meantime and now were empty, waiting for the new load. Three of these were equipped with round openings on the roofs, just the kind we needed. *We are all set*, I thought, *all we need is some merchandise to be loaded on them.*

Something wasn't going right, though. I watched with disappointment as workers came and started to close the heavy rolling side doors on these wagons. That meant they wouldn't be loaded up again. To my relief, though, they had left the last one open. At least one would be used. As if to prove my logic, I noticed a large van pulling up alongside the wagon.

I could not make out its cargo from the distance. Daylight was fading, and dark clouds were gathering also, threatening with another rainstorm.

I gathered up my courage and calmly walked toward the truck. When I was close enough, I stopped to light a cigarette. A nearby floodlight made the wooden crates clearly visible. I could see the travel tickets, with large, red letters exclaiming: "Export; from Romania to Iraq."

As I read this, I dropped my cigarette in my excitement. We'd gotten our chance! I started to run as fast as my legs could carry me, to let Lazlo and Michael know.

"Get up, guys; get up!" I hollered at them.

They couldn't understand my excitement, and they jumped up in a panic.

"What is it? What happened?" they asked, alarmed.

"What has happened, my friends, is that we have gotten the wagon that we need."

"That is impossible," Michael was amazed but incredulous.

"No, it isn't; it is right here at the station, being loaded to go to Iraq. We don't have much time. They can finish loading in an hour or two."

"We are in trouble," muttered Lazlo. "We ate all the canned meat and have no money to buy any more."

"That is the least of my worries now," I snapped at him. "If there isn't, there isn't. We can live without that. What's important is that we have water."

"But that can be dangerous, if we go without food," insisted Lazlo.

"Listen up, even if we had money, it would not make any difference. There are no stores nearby, and I am not going to let this last chance go, just because of my belly. If you don't want to come, Lazlo, I won't force you. I only ask that you lock the flaps after me, for I am going."

I did not wait for their answer and started to check the contents of the travel bag. I found everything in order, so I started to fill the water jug. By the time I was done, they were ready too.

"Well, did you decide?" I looked at Lazlo.

"Yes, I am coming too," he said, putting his hands out in a friendly gesture.

"Let's go, then," I answered, accepting his handshake.

As we reached the yard, I saw that the loading was already completed, and the wagon was locked. They were starting to back it up and move it toward the main rails, where it would be connected to the rest of the train.

"Do you see? We are almost late." I pointed at the wagon being moved. "Now listen, we will have to watch this car very carefully and follow it, until we know where it's taken. Once it is on the main track, attached to the rest of the train, you all know what to do."

Exciting minutes came next. It was not easy to keep track of the car. It was moved in a complicated pattern from rail to rail. A fine, misty rain started too, further reducing visibility. Finally, the car reached the main rail and was connected. After that, several other cars were moved and attached to the line. Our car ended up eighteen back from the big, double-diesel engine.

I knew our time was coming fast, for the mechanics were already checking the wheels and brakes.

"Wait for me here," I told my friends. "I'll go and put the bags on the cars."

"Do you need help?" they asked together.

"No," I said, "it's best if only one person goes." I did not wait for their answer, and I grabbed the bags and started to walk calmly toward the train. It was dark, and the rain became heavier, so I did not have to worry much about being seen. I found a suitable open car that was carrying concrete slabs. I hid the bags among them and returned to Lazlo and Michael.

"All set."

"I still don't understand why we can't hide somewhere in the wagons until the train starts." Michael sounded somewhat worried.

"Because, my friend, the police can examine the train at any time, and we would be found out. I don't want to risk anything now, in the last minute." I terminated the conversation forcefully.

Michael did not answer, which I took as a sign of agreement.

I felt sorry for him, for I sensed that he was a little afraid of clambering about on the roofs of the cars of a moving train. Yet, as a true friend, he had accepted his role. I was deeply touched and wanted to say something.

"Listen, Michael, what you are about to do for us is an unspeakably brave and valuable help. We could not get anywhere without you. I cannot give you anything in return, except the technique of the escape plan. You can follow us after we have made it. All I want to say is that we are going to be grateful for the rest of our lives." I finished my speech and offered my hand.

His eyes glistened as he reached for my hand.

"Boss, your plan and your handshake are more valuable to me than anything else in the world, for they mean that one day, I will be free too."

He wanted to say something else, but Lazlo interrupted, pointing at the train. We followed his hand, and we could see the stationmaster handing over the traveling papers to the engineer of the train.

"Boys," I said, barely able to conceal my excitement, "get ready. The train will start moving any minute now. Once more, be extra careful jumping on the train or crawling on the roof. Everything is slippery from the rain. Always follow me!" I wanted to continue, but the shrill whistles of the engine drowned my voice. The train started slowly with loud clanks of the cars.

"God help us. Let's go!" I said and started to run toward the train. The train was gaining speed rapidly, and I was worried about my friends. I had previous experience jumping onto moving trains. I made it easily enough, grabbing a handle rail and jumping on the steps at the same time. I was thrown against the wall of the wagon mildly, but it didn't matter much. I was on the train. I did not see Lazlo or Michael, but I hoped that they both had made it too. I did not have to wait long before they both slid down carefully from the roof. We were elated, though the action was just starting. Most of the dangers had still been ahead of us before we got inside the wagon. Because of that, I had left some time for us to rest before we continued.

Danger! I don't even want to talk about that. I still have nightmares about falling off the roof of the car. It is almost impossible to describe it. The train was running fast in the darkness of the night, swaying sometimes violently to the left or right. It was slow and risky to crawl on the top of the train from car to car. The roofs were wet and slippery. Twice, I almost slid off. The rain blowing into our faces made it difficult to see what we were doing. Besides that, the black diesel smoke was burning our eyes as if it were live embers.

My hands were swollen from the banging and bruising, and my mouth was bleeding. At the last leap from one car over to the next, I slipped and hit my chin against a metal ledge. I barely noticed all this, though. The only thought in my mind was to reach our wagon. I looked back to see if Lazlo and Michael were following. I was relieved to see they were all right, though somewhat behind. Thank God!

The wagon I had jumped on was number thirty-eight. I had climbed over seventeen so far. That meant I had only three more to go. I was overjoyed. With renewed strength, I started again, forgetting the dangers. As a result, I almost got thrown off at the next stronger sway of the train. I managed to hang on, but my heart was beating in my throat. "If you are in a hurry, you'll be late," says the old proverb. I almost became proof of it. Cooling off, I became cautious again. At times, when the train was turning, I laid on my belly, low and motionless. I only continued my crawl when the train was on straight tracks. As a result, I reached the twentieth car from the one I had jumped without any further problems. That meant I was on top of the eighteenth one from the diesel engine. That was our car!

Lazlo and Michael were somewhat behind, so I had time to fetch at least some of our baggage. It was in one of the wagons nearby. By the time I got back, they were already crawling on the roof of our wagon too.

"Long live justice," I greeted them.

"*Vivat; vivat*," they answered happily.

"Stay here. I'll be right back," I said, going back for the water jug. They wanted to come and help, at least one of them, but I said I didn't need it. I felt safer by myself. I came back in a short time, though it was hard to crawl using only one hand and carrying the heavy jug in the other. Why complain, though, if I were successful?

The important thing was to move on to the next step. We started right away. I took the key from the bag and asked Michael to shine the flashlight onto the flaps. I started to turn the iron bar that connected them. To my great irritation, it was not moving.

"Lazlo, come help me. This darn thing must be rusty from the rain."

Lazlo crawled next to me, and we tried with all our might together. It took the two of us quite some time, and then finally, one ... two ... three ... the connecting bar moved, but with the sound of something crashing. A piece of the tongue of the safety lock had broken off.

"We are in big trouble," Lazlo uttered, turning pale.

"It is trouble," I agreed, "but not a major one. By the time we reach the border, it will be rusty again, and then, if the guards notice it, they might think the loaders did it." I said this with deliberate carelessness. I knew full well that the broken tongue was a real problem, but I did not want Lazlo to get scared, and I did not want either one of them to back off now.

The time came to say good-bye to Michael—not even on a street, but on the roof of a speeding train, in heavy rain, in the middle of the night.

"Lazlo, say good-bye to Michael; our time has come."

He held onto Michael's hand for a long time, and then they embraced—not like friends, but like brothers.

"Take care of yourself, Michael, and thank you for everything you have done for us," he said. After a last handshake, he lowered himself into the wagon. I handed him the bags, and then it was my turn to say farewell.

"Before I say good-bye, listen to me once more. After you close the flaps, make sure that the connecting rod is screwed back in its lock. Then check the wire again, connecting the seals. As you see, there are three seals on every flap. If any of them break, let us know, because that means we have to get out of the wagon. After you are done, don't move around much on the roof. Slip off into the closest brake cabin, and stay there until the next stop where you will have a chance to get off the train. From there, you can take a passenger train home. Don't try to jump off the train while it is running! If you do this, I will slap you silly the next time we meet. Do you understand me?"

"Yessir, I understand, boss," he said, moved.

"Let's do it, then," I said, somewhat moved myself. We shook hands and then embraced in hope of a chance to see each other again, though nobody knew when.

I lowered myself into the wagon to meet my friend Lazlo. The flaps closed over us. We could hear Michael's efforts to close the iron bar. After a while, it stopped.

"I am done with everything," Michael hollered.

"God bless you," we yelled back.

"God be with you, and take care of yourselves," we heard one more time. For a while, we could hear the noise of him crawling cautiously on the roof, and then all became quiet.

We could not hear any other noise but the loud clacking of the wheels and the long whistles of the diesel engine. They sliced into the night, with a painful sound of someone crying for help.

My plan had worked! Many dangers still faced us, but at this point, they were hidden in the future. We were locked in the wagon, as if in an iron jail. No way out, unless someone opened it from the outside.

How long, for how many days, were we going to stay in this self-inflicted imprisonment? I couldn't tell, but I didn't really care either, for I knew that this was the only sure way to leave Communist Romania.

Our First Day Inside the Wagon

I was delighted that the first stage of my plan had been completed. They say, though, that sadness is the twin brother of happiness, and I certainly experienced their close relationship. I was aching for something I had left behind. I had left my loved ones, along with long years of my life—the experiences of my youth that were part of me, and would be impossible to forget. Wherever I'd go in the wide-open world, I would only be a half of a man. My other half would always be at home with the people I love, with whom I had shared good and bad, happiness and sadness until now.

Is freedom truly worth this sacrifice? I could not tell, since it was still the secret of the future. It would have to change the present first, and then the present turn into past before I could make that judgment. Right then, the present for me was darkness and danger until the train running through my days and nights would reach freedom for me. My real life would only start then. The sweet roads of freedom would be quite unknown to me, though. I would have to take my first steps tumbling about and holding onto things, like a little, innocent child learning to walk.

Dim light started to take over the night inside the wagon. The rain had stopped, and the pale rays of the rising sun streaked into the wagon through the ventilation holes. It was loaded only halfway full, with wooden crates in two layers. The second layer wasn't even complete; it was missing a few crates.

I didn't like this. It could only mean danger in two ways. It was quite possible that they would finish loading it at some other station. The other problem was the broken safety lip. This might prompt the border guards to open and check the car. I was worried about these and tried to come up with some solutions. *First,* I thought, *we can open a crate, get the stuff out, turn the crate upside down, and we can hide underneath.* This sounded good, but when we opened it, the first box was full of shirts. There was no way to hide them in the wagon. I was concerned and felt unsafe without a hiding place. Lazlo realized our predicament too, but he also had no idea what to do. We were sitting pensively, mourning our early rejoicing, when, looking at the unfinished second layer of crates, I had an idea. It hit me so suddenly that I yelled out in excitement.

"I've got it, Lazlo; I've got it!"

"What are you talking about?" He was perplexed.

"Do you see the narrow wooden slats nailed around the crates? That means they are not piled directly on top of each other. There is a space of the thickness of that slat between them."

"So, what has that to do with anything?" he asked uneasily.

"Don't interrupt; just listen up." I continued my explanation. "We will pry off eight of these slats from some of the crates. We'll put one back in the middle of the space, and then with the eight slats, we build a base for the crates of the top row. Then one of us will crawl into the empty space; the other hands in the bags, and then he will crawl in too. Now, listen! Once we are both inside, we can reach out between the slats and maneuver the last crate on top of us. Then we will be hiding in that space of about a cubic meter, and the guards will never guess that somebody is there instead of just another crate."

"This is terrific!" Lazlo sounded astonished.

"One other thing." I interrupted his exuberance. "We won't have to stay in that little cubby all the time. That would be rather uncomfortable. Impossible for several days. When the train is moving, we will come out. We will only hide there, when we feel it slowing down as it approaches a station."

"Hats off, boss! I tell you, you'll get far in life with that brain of yours." He praised my idea.

We started working on the plan right away. Everything worked as planned, and we laid down to rest, well pleased with ourselves.

Not much else happened on that first day, except that the wagon was disconnected at a station and moved around quite a bit before it was attached to another train. This went on with such jolts and bangs that we felt close to serious concussions.

The Second Day in the Wagon

During the second day, the wagon started to heat up. The sun was shining brightly, and the metal hull of the wagon was crackling as it was heating up. There wasn't enough air coming through the ventilation holes. Looking out through the hole, I could see we were going along a big river. I recognized the Danube. It brought back sad memories from the past. I was getting a little anxious, for I knew we were getting close to the town of Giurgiu. Giurgiu is a border town with reinforced border patrol. This is where the railroad bridge connects Romania and Bulgaria. Our fate would be played out there.

I told Lazlo the time had come to deodorize the wagon with the formaldehyde against the canine unit of the border guards. After soaking our clothes, the atmosphere inside the wagon became even more unbearable. We had to be careful with the water, we knew; still, we kept gulping it to help endure the heat and lack of fresh air in the wagon.

The train started to slow down. I looked out through the ventilation hole. I could not see much, but I could make out that we were in a large rail yard, and the train was going to stop soon. Quickly, we hid in our little cubby and pulled the crate over our heads.

The place was way too small for two people and the bags. We had to sit crouched over, with our heads bent way down. We stuffed the openings around us with wrapping paper from the opened crate, so if they shined a flashlight into the car, the missing crate from the bottom row would not be visible.

The train stopped, and we waited for several hours. It was just awful. My limbs were getting numb. I wanted to stretch my back, my neck, but it was impossible.

The heat started to become unbearable. We could hardly breathe in the small, tight spot. Lazlo had caught a cold during the rains of the previous days and was fighting back his cough. It was painful to watch him as he pressed his mouth against his knees, trying to suppress his cough. His face turned flaming red from the effort. I was terrified that he'd get a coughing fit just as they were examining our car, and we would be found out.

We could hear people yelling and dogs barking on the outside. With my flashlight, I checked my watch, and realized that had been waiting for eleven hours. Out status was getting worse, but this time, I had the problem. I had to urinate. In that tight little place, with my nerves all tense, however, I just couldn't do it. Lazlo was getting worse too. I was almost ready to suggest that we get out of the cubby, when I heard people talk right alongside our wagon. I squeezed Lazlo's arm, frightened, and started to pray.

From their conversation, we could gather that they were the border guards, coming to check the car.

We could hear them trying to slide the door of the wagon and arouse the dogs to sniff. One of them climbed on the top of the car to check out the flaps and their safety seal. I was so scared that the cold sweat made my clothes soaked, as if I had taken a swim. We squeezed each other's arms so hard, the pain was reaching my bone. Then horror struck.

The guard on the roof yelled out.

"Somebody is inside this wagon! Call the Comrade Lieutenant."

The next minutes were terrifying torture for the mind. After a short while, the lieutenant's voice came.

"What makes you think that somebody is inside, Sergeant?"

"A piece of the safety seal is broken off, Comrade Lieutenant," the sergeant answered.

"Open up!" ordered the lieutenant.

Oh, God, in my fright, I felt my heart beating in my throat as I heard the flap move. He was opening the one directly above us. I touched Lazlo and motioned to him to hold up his arms in support of the slats above us. If the sergeant jumped on the crates, they might break under his weight, and he would crash right into our hiding place.

We could hear him lowering himself carefully. Then he jumped. Time of reckoning!

The slats swayed some, with a squeaking noise, and we felt his weight on our arms. He was standing over our head for a while, shining his flashlight around the wagon. Thank God, the wrapping paper stuffed in the cracks prevented the light from shining into our little cubby.

"Did you find anybody, Sergeant?" somebody yelled from outside.

"There is nobody here," he hollered back.

"Walk around inside, and check out everything carefully," came the new command.

The sergeant got off the crate above us and walked around the inside.

"Well, did you find anything?" somebody yelled again outside.

"Nothing," he answered nervously. "Probably the idiots loading the car broke the seal. What do they care?"

"Come out, then, and put a new seal on the flap," ordered the lieutenant.

"Damn those lazy bums! They make extra work for us!" The sergeant was grumbling.

"We'll make out a report about this," the lieutenant answered.

As we heard the flaps being closed and sealed, in my elation, I felt close to heaven. Though the immediate danger had passed, we still could not leave our uncomfortable hiding place for a while. We could still hear the guards outside the wagon. They started to inspect the car. They checked the wheels and the brakes.

I shined my flashlight on my watch. We had been hiding for sixteen hours by then. *We must be ready to move out soon,* I assured myself.

But as they say, "trouble comes in clusters," so we weren't done yet. We heard arguments from outside.

"But believe me, Comrade Sergeant, the wheel does have a crack."

Hearing this, we almost fainted, though the real fright came only afterward. We heard the voice of the lieutenant again, rather annoyed.

"What is going on here?"

"Comrade Lieutenant, one of the wheels has a crack in it. This car cannot move out like this. The wheel could easily break."

"That's a problem, because this wagon has to connect with a train in Bulgaria." The lieutenant was swearing loudly.

"I'll try, Comrade Lieutenant," the head of the inspecting crew answered.

"Don't try it; do it! You've got ten hours for it." The lieutenant was really mad by now. "If you are not done in ten hours, we will have to load the stuff into another empty car, which we do not have right now. Do you understand? So get going."

"Yes, Comrade Lieutenant."

This made me really scared. I forgot every problem we had earlier. I didn't care how crammed we were in our hiding place. I didn't feel how much I needed to go. All I could think about was that if they couldn't weld the wheel, we would be unloaded right along with the rest of the cargo. Our chances were slim at best. Our only hope was that the welding would work.

Crouching in the tight hiding place was more and more agonizing, but we did not dare to come out. We knew that was our only chance, unless we were ready to give up altogether.

Hours passed, and we hadn't heard any sound from outside. I was scared that they had gotten an empty wagon and would start the reloading any minute.

It did not often happen in my life before that I was truly afraid, but this time, I was. Knowing full well the consequences of being caught, I was scared out of my wits. I was wringing my hands and occasionally banging my head against the crate above us. The condition of Lazlo did not improve either. He had coughed, muffled into his palms, a couple of times, no matter how hard he tried to suppress it. This really annoyed me, though I knew he could not help it. I shined my flashlight at him and almost started to cry. My friend was pale as wax and soaked in sweat. *He'll die,* I thought in a panic. With great difficulties, I opened the water jug and whispered into his ear.

"Drink a little water."

"No, no ... we have to be careful with the water."

"Don't you worry about the water; drink!" I ordered.

"Whatever you say," he agreed, and he tried to swallow a few mouthfuls in his crouched position.

I took out my handkerchief, wetted it, and handed it to him.

"Here, take this, and cough into this if you can't hold it back anymore. It's not much, but it might help a little." I tried to be empathic.

Lazlo lifted his blue eyes at me. They slowly filled up with tears as he said, "I am sorry, boss, I can't hold it back. I know it will be my fault if we get caught."

"That's enough, do you understand me? Stop it right now! It is not your fault. It is fate, over which we have no power." I wanted to go on comforting him, but stopped abruptly as I heard noises outside the wagon. I just squeezed his arm reassuringly.

The time has come, I thought. *They are starting to unload the car.* Still scared, I accepted this new blow from bad luck, which had been my regular companion for such a long time by now.

I started to pray silently, knowing that only a miracle could save us now. Blessed be His name, the miracle happened. We started to hear the hissing sound of the electric welding gun. Few musical instruments have a sweeter sound than that crackling, hissing noise we had heard. With tears in my eyes, I squeezed my friend's arm again in encouragement. I was grateful from the bottom of my heart. I knew it was through God's special grace that we were saved and were going to have another chance to live for another day.

The Third Day in the Wagon

We escaped from the great immediate danger, but our situation did not improve much. We still had to hide in the tight little cubby. If we tried to come out to stretch our limbs, we would have run the risk of someone on the outside hearing us moving the crates. So we suffered in our close corner, hoping that the welding would not take long and we would start moving soon.

Now I started to develop some problems. After several futile attempts, I still could not urinate. I became very nervous, fearing serious long-term damage. Lazlo tried to comfort me and calm me down, even tried to splash the water in the jug softly, hoping that the sound might induce me to action, but nothing happened. My body was just too uncomfortably tangled to do it.

On top of everything, we started to feel very hungry. We had not eaten for three days now.

My neck and my back were hurting from bending over. I felt as if I had been beaten up by a heavy club. My knees, pulled up and bent, were numb, and I felt as if millions of ants were parading around on my sole. Lazlo was more or less in the same shape, except he had no problem urinating.

We felt close to passing out, when the wagon moved with a sudden jolt. This gave us strength again to hold out a little longer. They started to push our wagon back and forth, so we knew they were putting together another train to go to Bulgaria.

With all the banging and bumping of the wagons, I got dizzy and felt my brains all shaken up. We still could not leave our hiding place, because we heard the guards moving around us, hopping up and down the wagon. I didn't want to risk losing everything now. We were so close to success. I was extra careful, for I had been scorched twice before, and I knew, this third time, I would burn to ashes. The inspection by the Bulgarian border guards was still ahead of us, and they were even worse than the Romanians.

I was not watching the time, but it was quite a while before we could finally hear the whistle of the diesel engine, signifying that the train had started toward the Bulgarian border. It was just a short ride, and we could hear the train crossing the bridge of the Danube. This bridge connects Romania and Bulgaria. We were finally leaving Romania behind. Communism rules, of course, in Bulgaria too—no freedom, no human rights; it was all the same, except the name of the country.

The train slowed down, then stopped. From the outside, human voices and the barking of the German shepherds were audible again.

I felt worse and worse. Burning pain took over the whole lower part of my abdomen, and the sharp jabs were so strong, I was close to fainting. I clenched my teeth, trying to hold back my moans. With my head swimming, I tried to stretch my limbs, but the crates were blocking me on every direction. Lazlo noticed my worsening condition and shined his flashlight into my face. I must have been a pretty nasty sight, for he looked really scared.

"This can't go on any longer," he said. "We must give up."

"Never," I whispered and grabbed his arm.

"But if you can't urinate, your bladder will burst! I can't take the responsibility for you getting seriously hurt, boss."

His voice was desperate. He started to rise, lifting up the crate above us with his back.

107

"Stay in your place, before I say something I will regret later," I said with as much authority in my voice as I could muster.

"But I can't watch you die," he whimpered, wringing his hands.

"Listen up; we have to stay here. If I do not make it to my freedom, you will. Then you will have to write down all the suffering we have gone through, for the whole world to know."

"I can't do that. I can't watch my best friend suffer and die without help. I just can't."

I was about to seriously tell him off, when our car started to move again slowly. Another series of pushing and pulling and banging started. My body was weakening, but my hopes were restored. I was sure we were moved closer and closer to the main tracks, which could only mean we were going to move out soon. Physically, I felt miserable. I was cramped, hungry, and in a great deal of pain, but I clenched my teeth and made a commitment that even if I'd be dead by that time, I'd make it into a free country.

God ultimately took mercy upon me, for things started to happen fast. We could hear the Bulgarian border guards inspecting the cars. This temporarily made me forget everything else. I touched Lazlo, for I could hear them checking out our car. *Now or never*, I thought, my heart beating wildly. After long minutes and unexplainable noises, we heard them talk in a language we could not understand. That was scary. *What is going on?* we wondered. We were greatly relieved as we we realized that finally, the noise was moving away.

Our fright and our physical and mental pain took several hours to subside, but we felt indescribable joy at the whistle of the diesel engine as we sensed the train starting to move, gaining speed quickly.

I did not have strength left to help Lazlo remove the crate from above our heads. When we crawled out, I was barely dragging my aching body. I pushed my face to the ventilation hole. How sweet the fresh air smelled. I could finally urinate, and though it was bloody, I knew I was going to be all right. Hugging each other, we were dancing in the middle of the wagon, forgetting even that we hadn't eaten in four days.

I am still amazed at our miraculous escape from certain death, for I know how close to it I had come. My heart is overflowing with gratitude toward God, because it was his blessed hands that saved me. I owe him my faithfulness for the rest of my life.

The Fourth Day on the Wagon

The train was speeding across Bulgaria, making only a few stops. We didn't have to hide because these were passenger rail stations, and the Bulgarian-Turkish border was still quite far away.

The weather turned very hot, and the iron hull of the car soaked up the heat. The temperature inside rose steadily, and we had to take gulps of the stale water frequently. We had to be careful with our water, though, because the jug was less than half-full by now, and we had no idea how long it would take us to get to the Turkish border. We tried to get fresh air through the ventilation hole, but we usually got more dust and dirt than fresh air. We were also very hungry. Our empty stomachs were aching. Lethargic and tired all the time, we tried to take long naps on top of the crates, but that was not easy either. The constant, loud rattle of the wheels was getting to us. Our future seemed bleak.

I wasn't too concerned about starving, for I knew you could live more than fifteen days without food. But I was worried about the water. I figured, no matter how careful we were, it wouldn't last longer than two more days. It was scary to imagine what would happen if we ran out, and the train wouldn't stop for days. In that case, we were sentenced to death, for the doors or the flaps on the roof of the car could not be opened from the inside. Lazlo had also acknowledged the gravity of our situation and felt that we were in God's hands. He, who had saved us so often before, was our only hope again.

I had an idea that seemed somewhat of a gamble with our lives, but I felt we had to try it. I explained it to Lazlo. I thought if we poured some of the formaldehyde on a piece of rag and held it under our noses, the smell might help us to fall asleep. I wasn't certain, of course, but I figured it might work. Lazlo agreed, so I soaked two pieces of rags and handed one to him, while I held the other under my nose. I tried to empty my mind of all thought and concentrate on sleeping.

What really happened after that, I don't know. The next thing I remember was that I woke up in the pitch-dark wagon with a colossal headache. I won't ever know, of course, whether it was the formaldehyde or simply the exhaustion that knocked me out for such a long time.

When I woke up, Lazlo was still sleeping. I let him. Dawn was breaking outside, so I figured we must have slept through half a day and a whole night. Finally, Lazlo started to stir. When he opened his eyes, he, too, complained of a bad headache. I took out our last drops of lemon concentrate and mixed them into our stale water. We drank a few mouthfuls. My head was pounding, and I knew that I wouldn't have the guts to use formaldehyde again as a sleeping aid, for fear of never waking up afterwards.

The Fifth Day in the Wagon

Our water supply was really low by now. I knew that no matter how miserly we used it, we wouldn't have any by the next day. I did not delude myself to believe that we would be in Turkey by then, since we had not even reached the border yet. The train was progressing steadily, but it stopped frequently, and sometimes for hours. Our predicament was grave, and our spirits sank. I didn't feel like even talking, and it seemed that Lazlo had nothing to say either. We were lying on the crates, idle and weak from starvation. The air in the car was stuffy with the terrible heat. The dirt and dust were caked onto our skin, which was sticky with the sweat and stink of the past five days. My brain was pulsating, and frightful thoughts were chasing each other in my mind. *Am I going to finish my earthly existence in this condition?* I tried to chase these thoughts away and guide my inner eye toward some visions of beauty, but my fear would not let me. The pictures of devilish prospects stayed stubbornly on the monitor inside my head.

Lazlo's worsening condition was also making me nervous. His cough had stopped, but his pale, colorless face indicated that he was close to pneumonia, if he didn't have it already. I felt his face and neck with one of my hands, touching my own neck with the other for comparison. My neck was hot from the heat inside the wagon, but his face and neck were burning with high fever.

I was sorry to see my faithful friend in this miserable condition. We had very little water left, but I couldn't bear to watch him suffer so. I made him drink as much as he could. I arranged our bag under his head as a makeshift pillow, then wetted a piece of rag and put it on his forehead. I knew I was using up my own water supply and that I wouldn't be able to take a drink again until the evening, but his life was at stake. What was my thirst compared to that? I had to follow the road I had chosen for myself. Oh, God! What would I have offered at this point for a sliver of bread and a glass of fresh, cold water? Five years of my life, probably. As the proverb says, the hungry pig dreams about acorns, and I could not chase pictures of unattainable things from my mind. I was also tormented by my conscience for my friend Lazlo, whom I had talked into this life-threatening adventure. He agreed to come of his own free will, it was true, but still, he did so on my suggestion. I looked at him, full of compassion; I wanted to say something encouraging, but he was fast asleep.

Carefully, I lifted the wet rag from his forehead. His fever had completely dried it, so I had to wet it again. It must have felt good when I put it back again, for his tortured face smoothed into a gentle smile.

I got up and looked through the ventilation hole. I could see the sun setting, and we were running along the seashore, accompanied by the monotone rattling of the wheels.

Further down the beach, I saw children playing happily. Some of them stood up and waved to the conductor on the train. I was stirred. I knew they were not waving at me; still, it gave me encouragement and faith. Life was worth fighting for. Those waving children calmed me down.

Peace returned to my mind, along with the hope that everything would be all right. From the vicinity of the sea, I judged that we must be near the Bulgarian-Turkish border. Daylight faded away, and I couldn't see anything through the narrow opening, so I lay down on the wooden crates. The fresh air inside the wagon cooled down rapidly, refreshing my body after the long, hot, sticky day.

I wetted the rag on Lazlo's head once again and felt, with relief, that his fever had dropped somewhat.

After that, I drank some water myself, but only a few drops, just to wet my mouth. We had very little water left—hardly enough for another day, if we used it frugally.

111

The Sixth Day in the Wagon

This day, Lazlo improved a great deal. His fever had dropped, and though he was still very weak, it was clear that the greatest danger had passed.

Everything seemed fine this day. The air outside had cooled off, and the fresh air was flowing in through the vent holes. Sounds of loud thunder were also rolling in. A storm was approaching. In a short time, we could hear the raindrops on the roof.

Lazlo, recovering from his fever, asked for water frequently, and I couldn't deny him. I was suffering of thirst too. My lips were cracked and my mouth dry, and though there was still some water in the plastic jug, I could not drink. I did not know how long this miserable journey would last, and I had to save water. What should I do? I was trying to think and plan ahead, but my brain was not working at full speed. The thirst and the long days of starvation clouded my mind.

I was lying idle on the wooden crates and would have liked to howl like a wounded animal.

Outside, the rain was pouring. The raindrops were drumming loudly on the roof and sides of the wagon. Listening to them brought back childhood memories of big storms, when I would carelessly run around outside in the rain, enjoying the stinging sensation of the heavy drops on my skin and getting home soaking wet, to the dismay of my mother. I would have loved to be outside again, surrendering myself to the delight of the strong, cleansing force of the rain, feeling it wash away six days of dirt and grime and freshening my tortured body.

Unfortunately, these were just dreams. I could think about them eagerly, but they were as impossible as reaching out to touch the stars.

Lazlo was asking for water again, and I was scared, realizing that we had hardly a liter left in the jug. It was also a substance barely qualifying for that name. After days of standing in the plastic container, it looked and smelled horrible; it reminded me of a swamp. It made you nauseous, and even for Lazlo, it was hard to swallow.

I was about to suggest that on the Bulgarian border we should give ourselves up, when I hit on a brilliant idea. I got to one of the containers, broke the top, and took out two shirts. I tore off the wrapping. Lazlo was following me with his worried eyes. It was clear that he couldn't figure out what was I doing.

I smiled at him reassuringly and said, "Don't worry, my friend, we'll get some water soon, if my plan works."

"Impossible," answered Lazlo softly, still weak from his recent illness, but he watched my actions with obvious interest.

I looked out through the vent hole to make sure the train was going through an uninhabited area. Luck was with us. Wherever I could see, there were only hills covered with dense forest. I whistled happily in my excitement. I took the two shirts, grabbed them by the collar, and stuffed them through the narrow hole. When I felt them heavy with the water, I pulled them back in. I yelled out for joy. Water dripped from them! I offered one to Lazlo, so he could wash off the dirt and grime of six days. The other one, I squeezed into the plastic container. We continued with this, washing ourselves thoroughly with the one shirt and collecting the water from the other.

Words cannot describe how refreshing this washing felt. We were still hungry and so weak, that a ten-year-old could have easily knocked us down, but the water we drank and the clean feeling of our body restored our spirits so much, we felt completely reborn.

Lazlo's condition improved unbelievably fast. He could get up and walk around in the wagon; happiness glowed on his face.

We were both exuberant and, forgetting everything, slapped into each other's hands, congratulating, carelessly celebrating our victory over our cruel fate. Our ecstasy made us forget the oncoming dangers a little prematurely.

The slowing down of the train brought us to our senses. I looked out through the ventilation hole and almost fainted. I saw several border guards in military uniforms walking along the standing trains on the tracks around us. Our train was moving very slowly, and I knew it would stop any minute. I ran to the bag in a panic and sprinkled the remaining formaldehyde all over the wooden crates, our bodies, and the sides of the car. I finished that and turned over the opened crate, and we barely had time to crawl into our little cubby. Just as we pulled the crate over our heads, the train stopped.

A long waiting period started again, with our twisted bodies crammed into the tight space. Everything was the same all over. The barking of the German shepherds and the yelling of the people from outside, the loud jolting and banging of the wagons, and the shrill whistle of the diesel engine filled the air.

The tapping of the rain stopped on the roof of the car, and I sadly realized that it meant the end of our cleverly devised chance to get water.

Our hiding place seemed more uncomfortable too. For some reason, I had a hard time breathing and felt sharp pains in my twisted limbs. Of course, I could not do anything. I had to endure, knowing that this would be our last trial. Lazlo was moaning softly next to me. He had serious stomach cramps, from hunger, and I warned him to try to be quiet, for I heard noises approaching the wagon. I could not quite make sense of it, though, because they came closer for a while, but then they faded away immediately, and there was no movement around the car for a long time. Long minutes passed, and I was worried that they had found some other mechanical problem again with one of the cars, and that might become our final downfall.

I was getting closer to panic when I heard the whistle of a diesel engine from the distance, and our wagon moved. It was crawling at an extremely slow pace for quite a while. Not being able to make any sense of this, I was getting really nervous. Then, finally, the engine gave out a few more whistles, and the train started to pick up speed.

We stayed hidden for about an hour after the train was running full speed already, without ever stopping again. *What does this mean?* I wondered. Finally, I touched Lazlo and said, "Lazlo, I think the train has gone through the Bulgarian-Turkish border."

"That's impossible; we haven't heard anything indicating the examinations of the wagon by the border guards," he said in disbelief.

"I agree, but I still think we are already in Turkey."

"I can't believe it. I just can't," he insisted.

"Let's find out," I said, and with my back, I lifted the crate above our heads.

I did this at just the right time. As I stood up, I could see through the ventilation hole. I yelled out so loudly that poor Lazlo dragged himself to me in a panic. The train was running through a small station without stopping, but as we sped away in front of the station house, I could see the fluttering red flag with the gold crescent moon and the star in one corner. I knew that flag! We were in Turkey! Oh, God! After all the suffering, I was out of Romania!

I was in a free country, where they were going to accept me as a political refugee, and after that, the road would open to the country of my dreams: America.

Happiness engulfed us. We were singing and dancing, as if we had been drinking some powerful booze instead of stale water for the past few days.

We drank all the water from the jug, sharing it like brothers, putting an end to our thirst.

The wise saying goes: "Don't celebrate until you have killed the bear." We learned the value of this one, too. We were free, but not quite yet. We started to realize this as the train ran through several stations in the next hours, without stopping anywhere.

It was afternoon, but the sun was still beating down hard on us in Turkey, and the inside of the wagon started to heat up unbearably.

We looked at the empty water jug and started to worry. In our exuberance, we had wasted all our water that we had saved so painfully at the beginning of the trip. As time passed, our hunger started to become harder and harder to endure, especially when combined with the thirst. We felt our bodies start to use up their own resources, disassembling themselves.

With hungry eyes, I looked out the window, hoping to see a station where we might stop. There was nothing. As far as the eye could see, there were empty, rolling hills.

Hours passed. The sun was setting. Its last rays were still beating the side of the wagon. I noticed a larger town in the distance. The train was turning toward it, and hope woke up in my heart. Maybe we would stop there.

We did not. The train ran through the station without slowing down a bit. I screamed as loudly as I could as we passed through, but nobody heard me.

How could they have, in the running freight train? And even if somebody had noticed, how could they have helped?

I realized sadly that our only chance was if the train stopped or slowed down considerably in a station. This only chance did not seem to come in a hurry. We ran through stations at such a speed, it was as if we were bound to run out of this world in one great stride.

Lazlo was lying on the crates, motionless. He seemed to have given up completely to starvation and thirst, ready to die. It annoyed me somewhat that he had given up so easily and accepted the defeat. I was not willing to even think about that yet. I was hurt by this, because I had thought him stronger than this. I wanted to scream at him: *"Snap out of it! Get up! Don't give up yet!"* but I held my tongue. I looked at him, and still seeing the sign of his recent illness, I thought it cruel to hurt him any more. It was painful, though, to accept that I had a partner, and still I had to struggle alone.

Late at night, while he was sleeping, I looked around in the wagon with my flashlight and tried to figure out a way to break open the wagon from the inside in case the train wouldn't stop for several more days. I racked my brain, but I could come up with nothing workable. The wagon could not be opened from inside by our own strength. Time was passing slowly, but my hunger and thirst were mounting fast. I checked my watch. It was midnight. I collapsed in the corner, and with tears in my eyes, I admitted that I might be free and out of Romania, but my real freedom was in the hand of God. He would decide about my fate. He would be my judge and decide if I was worthy to live in freedom or to die of starvation and thirst in a free country, but inside a closed wagon.

I accepted my fate, and I started to pray. I wasn't asking for help anymore. I just implored that he would take my beaten, torn, aching soul and admit it into his kingdom, where one does not have to struggle for freedom.

The Seventh Day in the Wagon

I woke up from my dream, where I was captured by border guards who were poking hot irons into my throat.

I looked around in the wagon, scared. It was still dark. I tried to feel my throat with my hand. There was no hot iron, but the burning sensation of thirst was closely competing with the pain of one.

Dawn approached and daylight seeped inside the wagon. My friend Lazlo was still sleeping. I was glad about that, because I knew when he woke, his first word would be, *"Water."* I wouldn't really mind if he could sleep through the whole day.

I was rather weak myself. My strong muscles, which I was always proud of, were now soft and flabby, due to my small stature and the long starvation. My former strength, known and admired by many before, had left me, as if I never had it. My legs got weak too. As I tried to get up and walk to the vent holes, they wobbled like Jell-o and almost gave out. I wondered how long it would take, even if I made it out of there, to get back my youthful strength and agility. I thought about it with a wry smile.

I looked out through the ventilation hole. It was early morning, but the sun was already strong and warm, implying another hot day. Dispirited, I tried to find some occupation for myself, after I was convinced that the train was running through long kilometers of uninhabited territories.

From the bag, I took out some thin wire and started to braid it to form a staff for a flag. When I was done, I took out a shirt, tore out the back of it, and attached it to the staff to make a flag.

I was hoping to use it if we got close to a station, and if the train slowed down enough. This might make us more noticeable, even if they couldn't hear us scream. I was passing the time this way, meanwhile still hoping that the good Lord would stop the madly running train.

The warmth of the sun's rays was increasing, and the temperature inside was rising. Lazlo woke up, and looked around, confused, as if he didn't know where he was. His first move was to reach out for the water jug.

"There is no more water, friend," I said, as if he didn't know.

"I know that," he answered in a miserable tone, "but I dreamed that jug was full."

"Then you had a better dream than I had. At least you could drink in your dream. I had a burning iron poked onto my throat in my dream," I answered, trying to make a joke of it.

"How can you still joke, boss, when we are so close to dying of thirst and starvation?" he asked in a lethargic voice.

"I know that too, Lazlo, but I won't start mourning for myself when I am only halfway there. Don't you forget," here, I raised my voice, "first, that we had freely chosen this road. Second, we are still a very long way

117

from dying of thirst. We should be able to live without water for at least two or three more days. Three-fourths of our body is water, so we still have some reserve, though using that up may not be a pleasant experience. Starvation, we shouldn't even worry about, since we would die of thirst way before we would starve to death. So, my friend, don't try to forecast anything terrible. Let's place our trust into God." I concluded my little speech somewhat nervously.

Lazlo did not answer. He had to accept that I was right. I really felt for him, but there was nothing I could do. I suffered just as much, or more, but I tried to hide it from him.

Time was passing hopelessly. Lazlo thought it best to close his eyes. I lay back on the wooden crates too. It drained my energy to stare at the barren landscape. The terrible heat was squeezing the last drips of enthusiasm out of me, and I slowly drifted into sleep.

I don't know how long I stayed in this half-sleep, half-fainted condition, but I was awakened by the whistle of the diesel engine. It seemed to come from a great distance. I sat up with confusion on my face. My head was swimming, and I felt that my hearing had weakened terribly. I could barely hear the rattling of the wheels. My eyes were burning from dryness, and every move of my eyeballs sent a sharp pain into my brain. My throat felt inflamed; my tongue swelled up in my mouth. I tried to collect some spit in my mouth, to swallow it and wet my throat some, but it was in vain. Strong spasms were attacking my stomach too. I felt as if someone was periodically kicking me in the belly.

I felt the train slowing down. I wanted to get up, to peek out of the ventilation hole, but to my great surprise, I could not. I tried to crawl on my hands and knees, and with considerable effort, I finally managed. When I finally reached the wall of the wagon, I pulled myself up and looked out. The train was approaching a large city and was slowing down gradually. Seeing this, I gathered all my strength and tried to wake up Lazlo. I could hardly manage.

"Large city, my friend! Very large city! Wake up; our suffering is over!" I was only able to whisper in his ear. His face lit up, and he tried to sit up but fell back.

"I cannot stand up," he sighed.

"Of course you can. Come, I'll help you." I supported him with my arms, and he finally managed to get up. We looked at the houses and the people walking on the streets with delight.

"This must be Istanbul," I said, and I stuck my homemade flag through the vent hole.

The train reached the station after agonizingly slow minutes, and it moved very slowly on the tracks.

I was waving my flag happily, and beating on the wall of the wagon with a piece of wood from the crates. With great delight, I saw that some railroad workers had noticed the noise and the flag and looked, puzzled, at our car. Finally, the train stopped on the first track.

On the platform, a large crowd was waiting for the passenger train. Several people noticed my flag or heard my banging and my cries. The crowd gathered around the train curiously. In a little while, a policeman came and moved the crowd back, away from the wagon.

The policeman started to talk to me in a foreign language. I did not understand anything and kept repeating, "We are Romania. We are from Romania."

A few railroad workers started to open up the wagon. It took them quite some time to do it. The door seemed to be stuck on something, but thank God, it finally opened, and with it, freedom opened up in front of us.

The policemen were waiting for us with cocked revolvers, since they had no idea who we might be. When they saw our conditions, though, they put their weapons away, embarrassed, and helped us get off the train. We could not say a word. We stood there and tears welled up in our eyes. We were free!

EPILOGUE

This is how my miserable seven-day trip with Lazlo ended—a trip I never regret I took. I have suffered a great deal conquering the difficulties of my escape from Romania.

The events I have described are all true. I did not add anything. This book is a faithful account of my sad life.

I know I deserved the success of my third attempt. I had suffered enough in Romania. But I also know that I owe my gratitude to God till the end of my life. Without his grace, his help in deadly dangers, I could have never succeeded.

At the present, Lazlo and I are living in America. I can finally say that there is peace in my heart. I lay my head on my pillow in tranquility, because both my body and my mind found the land of my childhood dream: America.

Oh, God, hallowed be thy name, and blessed be America, the country of real freedom!

PS—My other friend, Michael, escaped successfully from Romania about a year after we did. He now happily lives in Germany.

P.D.

FEARLESS AT ANY COST

The book *Fearless at Any Cost* recounts a real episode from the life of the author during the 1980s in Communist Romania, a country where the expansion and public adoration of Communism were holy laws. A country where contradicting Communism and its faithful followers were synonymous with death. A country where the spokesmen of religion or of human rights were persecuted. From this country, I, the author, tried to escape, longing for freedom.

My first attempt to escape was unsuccessful. I was caught at the Romanian border. In this book, I faithfully describe all the suffering and the inhumane treatment I was subjected to, such as the unfair punishment of hard labor only to try to break my spirit and my desire for freedom. Did they succeed? No.

I tried to escape a second time. Unfortunately, my second attempt failed also. This time, I wasn't captured, for I lost myself in a deadly swamp. This deadly swamp was my salvation, so I didn't fall back into the hands of the murderous Communists and didn't stand in front of another unjust court. This second failed endeavor almost broke my fighting spirit. But what choice did I have?

I was gambling with my young life, and I risked everything again with a third try. I knew this third one was going to be the last. Whether I made it or not, I wouldn't have another chance. For if I failed again, the protecting heroes of Communism would finish me.

At this time, luck was with me. My third attempt was the real thing. I succeeded, and finally, I achieved my long-awaited freedom.

In this book, I describe all the pain and suffering my family and I had to endure. Exciting complications, daring actions, overcoming deadly dangers—they are all here. I describe the seven days I spent in a locked freight car without any food—all the real events of my escapade.

In this book, the reader will find every reason to respect freedom and every reason to abhor Communism. One can understand how often are we frighteningly close to death and can hope for redemption only from God. One can understand why thousands upon thousands have risked their lives for freedom, and how that freedom is worth all the pain and unjust suffering.

In a Communist country, reaching for freedom seems as realistic as reaching for the stars. The book *Fearless at Any Cost* might bring tears into the eyes of the reader, until the happy ending, where he can sigh and say, "Thank God; after all that suffering, he reached his freedom."

PHOTOGRAPHS

From Left to Right: Myself, Mother, Sister, Father, and Brother

My Parents

My Parents

My Daughters, Claudia and Astrid

Claudia

Astrid

Myself and Sandi

My Daughter Holly

This Is The Last Picture Before My Final Escape.
From Left: Me with My Daughter, Astrid; My Sisters, Iboly and
Aranka; My Brother Andras; and standing, My Nephew, Jocoka

CPSIA information can be obtained
at www.ICGtesting.com
Printed in the USA
FFHW01n1533130718
47409364-50619FF